THE CAMPBELTOWN & MACHRIHANISH LIGHT RAILWAY

by

A. D. Farr

THE OAKWOOD PRESS

A humorous postcard of the railway produced by Martin, 14 Main Street, Campbeltown, in the 1920s.   *R.W. Kidner Collection*

Published by
The OAKWOOD PRESS
P.O. Box 122, Headington, Oxford

CONTENTS

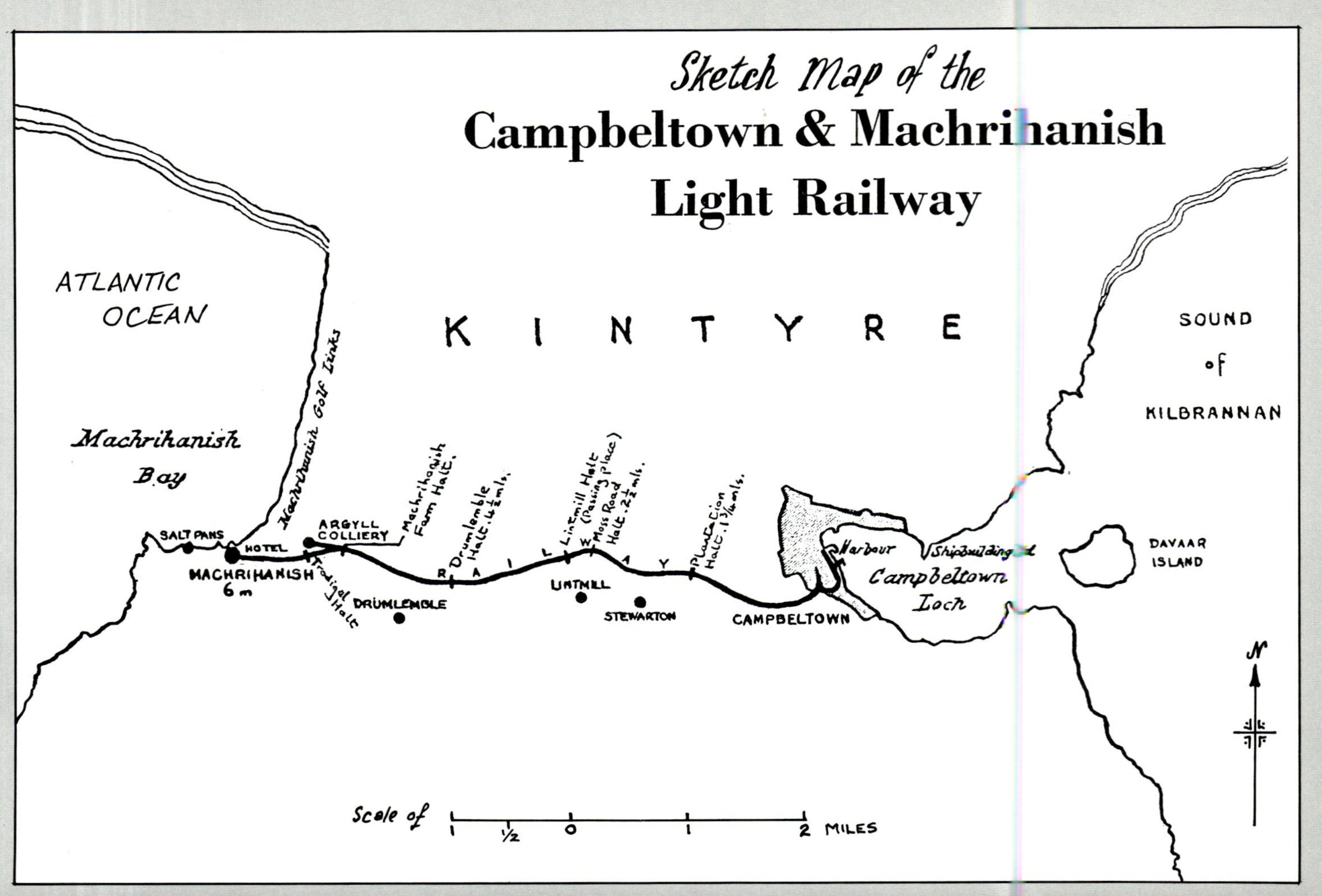

Sketch Map of the
Campbeltown & Machrihanish
Light Railway
ATLANTIC
OCEAN
Machrihanish
Bay
Machrihanish Golf Links
K I N T Y R E
SOUND
of
KILBRANNAN
SALT PANS
HOTEL
MACHRIHANISH
6 m
Trodigal Halt
ARGYLL COLLIERY
DRUMLEMBLE
Machrihanish Farm Halt.
Drumlemble Halt. 4 1/2 mls.
R A I L
Limemill Halt (Passing Place)
W. Moss Road Halt. 2 3/4 mls.
A Y
UNTMILL
STEWARTON
Plantation Halt. 1 3/4 mls.
CAMPBELTOWN
Harbour
Shipbuilding Yd
Campbeltown Loch
DAVAAR ISLAND
Scale of
1   1/2   0   1   2 MILES
N

Chapter 1

OVERTURE

Like voices of springtime to the glen
Like summer to the vale,
So is the news to Campbeltown
That I'm just gaun to tell;
For gloomy winter bleak and cold,
Nae mair we'll need tae fear,
We'll get our fuel cheap and good
Brought by the "Pioneer".

One of the endearing features of the British character is the love for lost causes and this is nowhere more evident than in the fascination evinced for the quaint, but struggling, narrow-gauge railways that were once found in the less accessible corners of the country. Built for cheapness in areas of sparse population and limited local industry they rarely made substantial profits and usually passed into oblivion with the advent of the internal combustion engine.

The narrow-gauge lines of Ireland and of Wales are well chronicled, as are some of the English lines and those of the Isle of Man, but in Scotland there was only one narrow-gauge railway (in the conventional sense) and that ran in an area so inaccessible as to have strong affinities with the outer islands. It has indeed been suggested that the Campbeltown and Machrihanish Light Railway was "remote from the world" and self sufficient in an almost unworldly way, with "operating methods reminiscent of the West of Ireland". Certainly it was a railway of character. The history of this railway has so far gone almost entirely unsung but here, nearly forty years after it closed, is its requiem.

The peninsula of Kintyre, a 45-mile-long strip of land which dangles down between the islands of Arran and Gigha into the approaches of the firth of Clyde, only narrowly misses being an island. Only a 1-mile-wide strip of land between west and east Loch Tarbert connects the peninsula with the rest of Argyll. Mountainous for most of its length, there is a short transverse plain near the southern tip, running from the sheltered waters of Campbeltown Loch in the east to the open Atlantic at Machrihanish in the west. It was along this 6 miles of fertile plain, never rising more than 50 or 60 feet above sea level that the Campbeltown and Machrihanish Light Railway ran. The Kintyre peninsula has a remarkably fine climate, bathed as it is by the Gulf Stream to the west, and sheltered by the firth of Clyde to the east, and palm trees, azaleas and multi-coloured hydrangeas grow in the gardens of Campbeltown; but it was for its coal and its distilleries that this beautiful outpost of the western highlands was important, and it was for the transport of the coal that a railway was first built to connect the old Argyll Colliery with Campbeltown.

Perhaps no railway in Britain was as isolated as was this short narrow-gauge enterprise, for Campbeltown is probably one of the least accessible towns on the mainland. Closer to Ireland than Glasgow, the nearest railway neighbour was the Ballycastle section of the L.M.S. (N.C.C.) 25 miles away in Ireland, while by land the nearest railhead was at Oban, some 90 miles away, and by road to Glasgow (the nearest city of consequence) a journey of 134 miles is involved via Inveraray and Arrochar. In the summer months three boats a week come to Campbeltown from Glasgow and there is today a daily plane from Abbotsinsch. The first motor car was seen in Campbeltown in 1898, but in 1906 when the passenger line was opened, the south tip of Kintyre was even more isolated than it is today.

Campbeltown is a pleasant small town, centred around its harbour—although in 1939 one author said of it that visitors "pass through Campbeltown as quickly as possible. There is nothing there to attract them; and indeed there is a good deal to repel them. The ragged children playing in the paper littered gutters of the Long Row, the toughs by the quayside, and the lifeless distilleries with their shuttered windows, are signs of the typical squalor and bleakness of a depressed Scotch town." This is certainly not the picture seen by visitors today, who admire the home town of Burns' sweetheart—Bonny Mary of Argyll. A more balanced view was given in the Turbine steamers handbook of 1907, the year after passenger trains started. "There is of course the full complement of tall chimney stacks, as becomes the home of twenty odd distilleries, but as a set off against this utilitarian plenitude there is perhaps a commensurate number of imposing church spires." But perhaps the greater beauty is to be found at Machrihanish, where probably the finest natural golf course in the country extends fully 6,000 yards along the shore, commanding a magnificent view of the bay where the glorious long sandy beaches, stretching for 3½ miles, entice numbers of holiday makers during the warm days of summer. Along the cliffs there is a magnificent walk of about 12 miles southwards to the Mull of Kintyre, one of the "Land's Ends" of Scotland, with its lighthouse and view of the 13-mile-distant Antrim coast. It was partly the attractions of this lovely western coast that caused a passenger-carrying line to be built for the tourists coming "doon the watter" through the Kyles of Bute from Glasgow.

ALONG THE LINE

Let us look at the line as its first passengers saw it in 1906. Starting from Hall St. in Campbeltown the line ran for a short distance along the side of the loch, after which it began to ascend to its summit, from which an attractive view of the town and loch was to be seen. Passing over a ridge about 100 ft. above sea level the train then descended towards the low ground known as the Laggan. Ahead could be seen the towering mast of the wireless telegraph station at Machrihanish, and the tourist may have caught a first glimpse of the Rhinns of Islay, far out on the Atlantic. Crossing the public road the line passed at a little distance the two small villages of Stewarton and Lintmill, passing through low ground which was formerly a peat moss and in which the stumps of gigantic oak trees of a bygone age were still to be found. At a still earlier period the whole of this ground must have been under water, a depression of 50 or 60 ft. being sufficient to allow the sea to flow right across from Campbeltown Loch to Machrihanish Bay. The land has risen to its present elevation by successive stages, at each of which a terrace of sand and gravel marked the shore line. One of these terraces was cut through by the railway, just beyond the end of the peat moss, displaying a profusion of sand and well-worn pebbles.

On the left, at some distance could be seen the mining village of Drumlemble, with its schoolhouse, post office, and mission hall. Looking seawards the passenger then obtained, if the weather was favourable, a more complete view of the two principal islands of the west; Islay, a long mountainous island, seemingly cut in two with the low neck of land on which stands Port Ellen completely hidden beneath the horizon and, to the north the lofty "Paps" of Jura. Half a mile to the south the train passed the small ruined church of Kilkiven, dating from pre-Reformation days and with ancient carved Celtic tombstones. To the right stood the tall chimney and winding-pulleys of the only colliery in Argyll and, just beyond this a little plain called Machaireionan, where in the 10th century a battle was fought between Scots and Danes. Another battle was fought on the slopes beyond Crosshill in 1652, when the fiery MacDonalds made one of their rare truces with the Campbells for a joint assault on the fort held by Cromwell's men. Finally the train passed behind a group of "modern villas" to emerge at the terminus behind the Ugadale Arms Hotel a few yards from the shores of the Atlantic.

The railway that ran in this fair and pleasant land was, in more ways than one, unique. It was the only narrow gauge surface line in Scotland (despite starting as a colliery line, where the narrow gauge usually went below the surface. Perversely the only other Scottish narrow gauge line, the Glasgow District Subway, although being entirely a passenger carrying concern, went underground.) It was also by far the most isolated stretch of public railway in Britain—90 miles from the nearest railhead— and the only Scottish Light Railway to own its own rolling stock.

It all started like this . . .

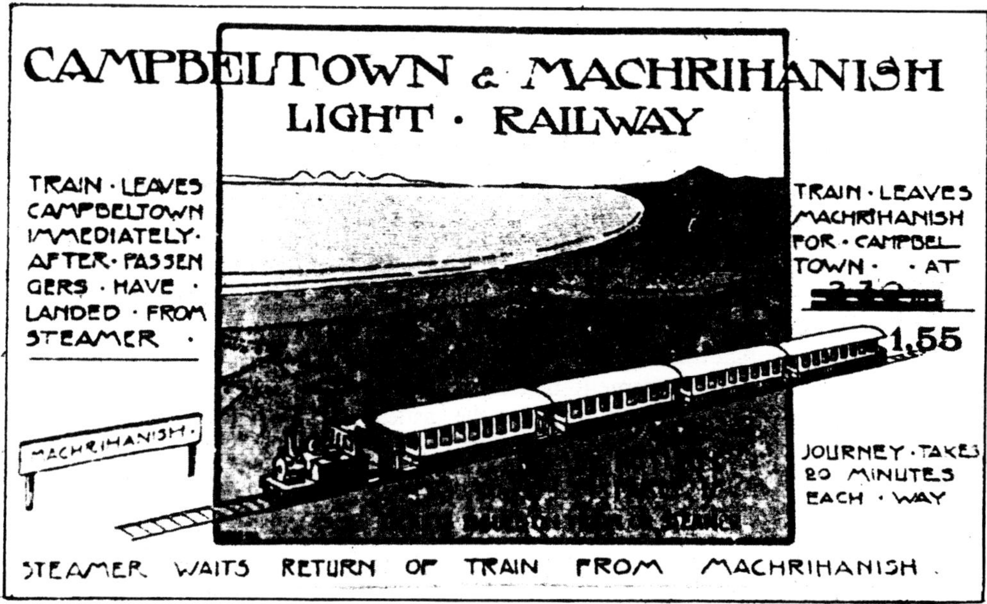

Chapter 2

Colliery Days

> Her coals will bless the poorest hame,
> And cheer the humblest hearth,
> Although in other parts they're dear,
> No more we'll dread their dearth.
> The coals that come frae other lands
> Let them be cheap or dear,
> We'll rather hae oor hielan' coals
> Brought by the "Pioneer".

Coal—and a Canal

In the south-west corner of Kintyre, in the plain behind Machrihanish, is found the only coal in the west highlands, stretching out under the sea to the west and forming part of the same carboniferous strata which extends from the east of Scotland to the Antrim coast. "Admittedly (the coal is) of poor quality," said one of the owners of the pit in 1906, "but it is useful for steam raising." It must also have been useful to the Irish, for it was thence that much of it was exported from Campbeltown.

How the coal first came to be discovered is not known, but as early as 1498 it was being worked for use in the castles maintained in Kintyre by King James IV, who had sent a certain John Davidson—*"a collman to pass through Kintyre to verify if colys may be wonnyn there"*. Three centuries later the output had become "considerable" and from about 1763 some of it was being sent by horse and cart to Campbeltown for use by the many distilleries. The countryside was generally flat, however, and the current interest in canals suggested the cutting of one for this purpose. Accordingly, in 1773 a survey was made by the great James Watt. Construction was begun in 1783, with Watt as the engineer, and the canal was in operation by 1794.

Three miles in length, the canal ran from the Mill Dam by the colliery to Campbeltown, where it terminated close to the present site of the gasworks. It has indeed been suggested that these works were built there in order to gain the benefit of being "contiguous to the canal". There were no locks, and two barges plied its length carrying first some 40 cart loads of coal a day to Campbeltown, where it sold for 2s. 7½d. per load, or 7s. 10½d. per ton.

The extent to which the canal was used or cared for seems doubtful.

Certainly older inhabitants of Campbeltown used to remember skating on it in the winters of their youth. It had fallen into disuse and been virtually abandoned by 1856 and when, about 1875 the colliery changed hands, the new owners (the Argyll Coal and Canal Co.) found it choked with weeds and difficult to clear. It was soon decided that a better outlet for the coal was needed and in the Company's prospectus of 1875 it was stated that a railway was to be built.

THE MINERAL LINE

In building the railway the intention had been to follow the line of the old canal, but this was not done and the two eventually coincided only over a distance of some 740 yds. An article in the *Campbeltown Courier* of 6 May 1876 said that locomotives and rails were expected the following month and during that July the works were commenced. Under the heading "THE NEW RAILWAY" the *Courier* reported on 29 July that "Operations were commenced this week for cutting out the new line of rails in connection with the Argyll Coal & Cannel [*sic*] Company's works at Trodigal. The ground has already been broken along different parts of the line, and we understand a large force of navvies have arrived in town who will be employed at the excavations." Three weeks later a brief note recorded that ". . . on Tuesday the schooner W.M.J. of and from Briton Ferry, Wales, Captain Lloyd, arrived here with the rails for the new line, and these will be laid down as soon as possible".

The railway ran from the pits to the coal depot in Campbeltown at the east end of Argyll Street—a distance of about 4¼ miles, which was later extended to 4·7 miles in 1881.

The gauge of the line was 2 ft. 3 in. and the rails were flat-based of 30 lb. per yard, in 21 ft. lengths, spiked to wooden sleepers spaced 3 ft. apart. The maximum gradient was 1 in 35 and the sharpest curve of 150 ft. radius, of which it was said that "a considerable amount of grinding is experienced in traversing this curve". Writing in 1902 the engineer, Mr. T. L. Galloway said, "There are no other sharp curves and, if it had not been for this one, it might have been practicable to have used heavier locomotives with 6 wheels coupled, which would no doubt have greatly increased the capacity of the railway". There were a number of level crossings, all originally gated but subsequently left open, protected only by cross trenches to keep cattle and sheep off the line.

The original locomotive was an 0–4–0 tank engine named "Pioneer", built by Andrew Barclay of Kilmarnock and delivered later in the year. The *Campbeltown Courier* of 11 November 1876 reported that "On Tuesday one of the new locomotives for the railway now being constructed for this enterprising Company arrived per steamer Kintyre, and was taken to the coal work, Drumlemble; where it will in a short time be set in motion."

Work went on through the winter and on the following 21 April the *Courier* reported "The new line of railway between Drumlemble and the town . . . is now completed. The waggons, however, have not yet arrived from Glasgow although they are expected daily, and on their arrival the traffic between the works and the depot will commence." In the event it was a month later that the wagons did arrive, on the steamer "Gael", which docked at Campbeltown on Saturday 19 May. By the following Wednesday they were in "full working order and loads have been brought to the town daily since". The date of opening of the line for traffic was therefore Wednesday 23 May 1877.

With the line in operation the price of coal at Campbeltown Depot on and after Monday 28 May was quoted as:

Household coal	8s. per ton
Triping	4s. 2d. per ton
Dross	2s. 6d. per ton

In 1881, however, the Kilkivan pits became exhausted and Messrs. J. and T. L. Galloway opened the new Drumlemble pits some half a mile farther west. The railway was then extended to this new "Argyll Colliery" and business became so brisk that in 1885 a second locomotive was bought from Barclays, an 0–4–0 saddle tank named "Chevalier" which was destined to become the longest-lived engine in Kintyre.

The cost of constructing the railway had not been high—about £900 per mile, excluding the cost of embankments, cuttings and bridges. The figure was broken down thus:

	£	s.	d.
Rails at 40 lb per yard, 63 tons at £5	315	0	0
Fish Plates, 48 cwt. at 7/-	16	16	0
Bolts, 17 cwt. at 16/-	13	12	0
Sleepers, 2,200 at 1/4	147	0	0
Spikes, 40 cwt. at 12/-	24	0	0
Stobs, 3,520 at 4d.	58	13	0
Fence Wire and Staples	12	0	0
Forming, 1,760 yards at 1/6	132	0	0
Ballasting 6′ × 1′ = $\frac{2}{3}$ c.yd. per lin. yd. 1,173 c.yds at 1/6	88	0	0
	£807	1	0
Contingencies, say	92	19	0
	£900	0	0

In 1897 a new company was mooted to take over the colliery under the name of "The Campbeltown Coal Company", and it was this company's wagons, bearing the initials "C.C.C." that were to become such a familiar sight to thousands of visitors during the ensuing 30-odd years. In its prospectus the company listed, amongst assets to be taken over, the $4\frac{1}{2}$ miles of railway, two locomotives and eighteen wagons. That business continued to increase is shown by the purchase of a third locomotive "Princess", a 0–4–2 side tank design purchased from Kerr Stuart of Stoke on Trent. Maybe she was needed urgently, for delivery was made within 7 weeks of placing the order; nevertheless this was to be the only locomotive on the line not from the Barclay stable. The old "Pioneer" had had a heavy life and it was not long after the appearance of "Princess" that she was laid up. Although taken over by the Light Railway Company in 1906 she was at that time described as being "no longer in service and is stored away at Drumlemble".

About 1902 there was a local dispute which caused the C.C.C. to consider diverting the line of the railway, but this was eventually settled and, although the renewal of lease to the company in that year required them to build a line on the route of the old canal, this was not done. At about this time too the old track was showing definite signs of wear, with weaknesses at the rail joints which were treated by increasing the number of sleepers to nine (each 4 ft. 6 in. x 9 in. x $4\frac{1}{2}$ in. and creosoted) per length of rail with closer spacing each side of the rail joints. The rails also were being replaced by 40 lbs. per yard lengths in some places.

The cost of working the line at this time was not very high. A figure of around £150 per annum was estimated for upkeep repairs and purchase of locomotives and wagons, this being a "variable and uncertain quantity". This figure was then taken into account in the cost of hauling 22,000 tons of coal over the 4·7 miles of the line as follows:

	£
Drivers' wages,	144
Surfacemen's wages,	98
Coal for locos., 460 tons at 8s,	184
Upkeep of rolling stock,	150
Renewal of rails, etc.,	50
Renewal of sleepers,	56
	£682

The net result was a cost of "rather less than $7\frac{1}{2}$d. per ton for the total distance, or slightly over $1\frac{1}{2}$d. per ton per mile".

The year 1901 had seen the introduction of the new turbine steamer "King Edward" to the Clyde and this was joined in 1902 by a sister ship "Queen Alexandra". These two turbine steamers with their smooth running and high speeds revolutionised the Clyde tourist trade and brought increasing numbers of day trippers to Campbeltown where, during their brief sojourn ashore, many of them were conveyed to Machrihanish, "to the shores of the Atlantic", by horse-drawn carriages. Although the railway had hitherto been purely a private and industrial one serving the colliery, its potential for development into a passenger line also, to serve this new tourist trade, must have been obvious to all concerned. Further, there would be obvious advantages in handling the coal if the line were to be extended to the New Quay in Campbeltown, so as to allow direct transfer from the railway to the boats which were increasingly taking it for export. Consequently talks took place between the Galloways (owners of the colliery), the builders of the turbine steamers (Denny's of Dumbarton), the local coal and distillery interests, and other interested parties, and these culminated in the formation of an "Argyll Railway Company" which was to acquire from the Campbeltown Coal Co. Ltd., the existing mineral railway, and to extend it to the harbour at Campbeltown and to the Golf Links at Machrihanish.

Chapter 3

PAVING THE WAY

Oh! Have ye heard the news, my frien'?
About this company, I mean
They say they're going to lay a line
And ca't the Hielan' Railway.
To Belfast trip no more we'll go,
Nor yet to see Ayr cattle show,
For better sport we'll have, you know,
Upon our Hielan' Railway.

Conversion to Passengers

In May of 1904 an application was made to the Light Railway Commissioners by the Argyll Railway Company Limited for an order to construct a Light Railway—or rather, four railways—between the New Quay in Campbeltown and a point near the Ugadale Arms Hotel at Machrihanish. It was proposed that the Argyll Railway Co. "and all other persons and corporations who have already subscribed to or shall hereafter become proprietors in the undertaking . . ." should be "united into a Company for the purpose of making and maintaining the railway . . . incorporated by the name of the 'Campbeltown and Machrihanish Light Railway Company'." The legal "domicile" of the company was to be in Glasgow and the first five directors were to be:

Col. John M. Denny of Messrs. Wm. Denny, Shipbuilders, Dumbarton.

James Wood, coalmaster, of Glasgow.

James J. Galloway, Engineer, of Glasgow.

James Ferguson, a distiller, of Glasgow.

and one other.

The four sections of railway authorised were:

No. 1. "4 furlongs 6 chains or thereabouts in length" running from the new passenger terminus at Hall Street in Campbeltown, "opposite the Christian Institute" along the foreshore to a junction with railway No. 3 "at a point 14 chains or thereabouts from the Campbeltown terminus of the existing miners' railway used by the Campbeltown Coal Company Limited".

No. 2 measured "1 furlong or thereabouts in length" and linked railway No. 1 with "the north-east extremity of the New Quay". This short branch was for the more convenient trans-shipment of coal.

No. 3 was "4 miles 5 furlongs 7½ chains or thereabouts in length" and was to be "partly upon the line of the said existing mineral railway commencing at the depot of the said Campbeltown Coal Company Limited following generally in a westerly direction the line of the said existing mineral railway and terminating at the colliery sidings of the said Coal Company at Argyll Colliery". This was essentially the existing line.

No. 4, "7 furlongs 6 chains or thereabouts in length", was to run from a point "1 furlong 7 chains or thereabouts" from the terminus of railway No. 3, and after crossing the main road, ran to its terminus "at or near a point 3 chains or thereabouts measured in a south-westerly direction from the south-west corner of the Ugadale Arms Hotel".

The total effect of all this was to provide a railway with an authorised track length of 6 miles 649 yards, which ran from Campbeltown to Machrihanish directly, apart from spurs to the colliery near Machrihanish and the coal depot at Campbeltown. The authorised gauge was 2 feet 3 inches and the motive power was to be "electricity steam or such other motive power as the Board of trade may approve", although it is interesting to note that the report of the Light Railway Commissioners for 1904 stated that the proposed motive power was to be "electric". Perhaps this was a Stationery office misprint, for the following year's report got it right and said "steam or electric". The works were to be completed within five years.

The usual Light Railway restrictions were to be imposed, including an overall 20 m.p.h. speed limit, with reduced speeds on steep gradients, sharp curves and within 300 yards of an ungated crossing. The maximum charges would not exceed 3d. per mile first class and 1d. per mile third class, with a permitted minimum charge as for 3 miles. Rails to be used would be of not less than 40 pounds per yard weight and the only signalling anticipated was at crossing places. A local inquiry into the application was held at Campbeltown on 28 September on behalf of the Light Railway Commissioners who duly approved the scheme and submitted it to the Board of Trade on 28 December.

On 8 May 1905 "The Campbeltown and Machrihanish Light Railway Order 1905" was made, and given under the Seal of the Board of Trade. This order authorised the line on the terms outlined above, to be capitalised by twenty-six thousand shares of one pound each, the paid-up amount being five shillings per share. The Order provided that when two-thirds of the authorised share capital had been issued and subscribed, interest not exceeding £1,500 could be paid out of Capital at a rate of 3 per cent while the railway was in course of construction.

The promoters must have been confident of obtaining their Order for within a month, on 5 June, a prospectus was issued inviting subscriptions for 23,000 Shares "at par, payable on application at 2s. per Share and on allotment 3s. per Share, and the balance as required at intervals of not less than three months". The list of applications was to close after less than a week, "on or before 10th June 1905". It was explained that 13,050 Shares had already been applied for, leaving 9,950 available for subscription, and that the Company had power to issue Debenture Stock to the extent of only £2,000, although a later Board of Trade Order dated 15 May 1908 increased this to £8,500. The Company's Office had been established at the office of their solicitors at 150 St. Vincent Street, Glasgow, and T. Lindsay Galloway, C.E., of Glasgow was named as Engineer.

Railway prospectuses were ever a source of delightful entertainment, in the high-flown prose and fulsome expectations which they contained, but by 1905 the years of "railway mania" were long since past and few people had any illusions left about the ready supply of quick profits offered by the early lines. Nevertheless, the author of this latest extravaganza made a noble attempt to follow the literary style embodied in the prospectuses of his predecessors of Glen Mutchkin *et al.*—and so well did he succeed that reading it, even over sixty years later, one can hardly see how it could fail.

After explaining the route and purpose of the line it went on to explain that "Machrihanish, with its attractive Golf Links, is a rapidly rising seaside resort, and the opening of the Railway should greatly develop it from a residential standpoint". Fair enough—even though the author couldn't have foreseen the cluster of prefabs which were later to be built on the site of the Machrihanish station, and the local storm that this would raise. That the tourist trade was the hub of the matter was then made clear, as the prospectus continued. It was explained that "large numbers of Passengers travel during the summer season to Campbeltown by the splendidly equipped steamers of 'The Turbine Steamers Limited' and other Companies, and hitherto Passengers by the steamers, desirous of going to Machrihanish have driven across from Campbeltown in brakes, but this mode of transit is very slow and insufficient". The number of passengers involved was dealt with very subtly, it being stated that the number carried to Campbeltown by the Turbine Steamers "during the seasons 1901, 1902 and 1903, was 135,880, of these, about 22,000 were booked through to Machrihanish". Now although the figure of nearly 136,000 looked impressive at first sight, the fact remained that only just over 7,000 a year were travelling to Machrihanish and could therefore be reasonably counted as a basis for trade. Beyond that was mere speculation. At 1d. per mile (there only being third-class accommodation actually provided) the return fare was set at 1s., and that meant an income of

ORDER

MADE BY THE

LIGHT RAILWAY COMMISSIONERS,

AND MODIFIED AND CONFIRMED BY THE

BOARD OF TRADE,

AUTHORISING THE CONSTRUCTION OF A

LIGHT RAILWAY IN THE COUNTY OF ARGYLL FROM CAMPBELTOWN TO MACHRIHANISH.

Presented to both Houses of Parliament by Command of His Majesty.

LONDON:
PRINTED FOR HIS MAJESTY'S STATIONERY OFFICE,
By DARLING & SON, LTD., 34-40, BACON STREET, E.

And to be purchased, either directly or through any Bookseller, from
WYMAN AND SONS, LTD., FETTER LANE, E.C.,
and 32, ABINGDON STREET, WESTMINSTER, S.W.;
or OLIVER & BOYD, EDINBURGH;
or E. PONSONBY, 116, GRAFTON STREET, DUBLIN.

1906.

Price 3½d.

Cover of the Light Railway order

only about £370 per year as far as the tourist traffic was concerned. Not much upon which to base a railway. Nevertheless, the prospects for improvement existed for, as the prospectus said: "At present the steamer arrangements permit Passengers to remain only a very short time at Machrihanish, and it is expected that with the speedier and more comfortable mode of travelling by the Railway, the steamer service to Campbeltown will be increased and otherwise improved, and that many more tourists and visitors will avail themselves of the Railway to Machrihanish. The present mode of transit between Campbeltown and Machrihanish seriously hampers the development of the latter place as a Golfing and Residential Resort." In retrospect, over half a century later, one may quietly chuckle, for even today the poor traveller only gets one hour at Machrihanish if arriving on one of the thrice-weekly turbine steamer visits, and the "speedier and more comfortable mode of travelling" promised in the prospectus was never more than an average $12\frac{1}{2}$ miles per hour on slatted wooden seats.

The tourist trade was not, of course, to be the only source of revenue and the development of "a considerable amount" of local passenger, goods and farm traffic was anticipated, as "in Campbeltown there is a population of over 8,000, and the Railway will run through the finest agricultural part of Kintyre".

The financial basis of the whole project of course was the mineral traffic, the line being essentially a development of the existing colliery lines. An agreement had been made with the Campbeltown Coal Company by which the latter was bound to send all its traffic over the Railway at a fixed rate of 2d. per ton per mile. The improved facilities to be provided by the extended line were expected to raise the daily shipment from 150 tons to 300 tons, and allow "at least 70,000 tons per annum of Coals and other Minerals" to be ultimately carried to Campbeltown, mainly for shipment elsewhere. Sadly, the estimate of workable coal available in the Argyll fields was over-optimistic, a recent Royal Commission being quoted as saying that it *should be sufficient to last for generations*". Alas, the seams are now worked out and the pits closed for good. Further prospects were foreseen for developing the export of Fireclay which had been "tested for brickmaking with satisfactory results".

The Campbeltown Coal Company had agreed to sell their existing railway, as it stood, complete with locomotives, etc., for only £4,500, and further to subscribe for 6,500 shares in the Railway Company.

The finances envisaged were of the usual over-simplified type to be found in railway prospectuses:

"The total Capital outlays required for constructing and working the Railway by means of steam traction have been estimated as follows:

	£
Permanent Way	14,237
Rolling Stock	2,576
Signalling Apparatus	900
Land, Cost of Obtaining Order, Working Capital	6,287
	£23,000

"The Revenue to be derived from the Railway has been estimated as follows:

TRAFFIC

	£
Passengers	1,300
Minerals	1,250
General Goods, Parcels, Luggage, Mails, &c., ...	300
	£2,850
Estimate of Cost of Working, Including Upkeep of Plant	1,531
Estimated Profit	£1,319

Which, on a Capital outlay of £23,000, shows 5 per cent, with a margin for contingencies or additional dividend." In the event the railway very rarely paid any dividend, and then it never exceeded 3 per cent.

As has been noted it was proposed to raise only £23,000 of the Company's authorised capital of £26,000 and it was pointed out that, as the mineral traffic would continue to be carried over the existing line until the passenger traffic started, the Company would begin to earn revenue at once.

The Permanent Way

The line to be built was of course a very simple one, single throughout apart from the two short spurs near either end (the Campbeltown one forming a reversing triangle), a run-around loop at each terminus and a passing place at Lintmill. The track was laid using mainly flat-bottomed rail weighing 50 lb. per yard on ash or broken stone ballast, and tramway-type flanged rail for the road-railway sections. A few short lengths of line had rails of 40 lb. per yard, and there were 12 creosoted Baltic redwood sleepers (each 4 ft. 6 in. x 9 in. x 4½ in.) per 30 ft. rail. The rails were attached to the sleepers by "fang bolts" at the ends and by spikes at intermediate points, and were connected by fishplates. At the sharpest curves certain deviations from the original track were made to conform to Board of Trade requirements, especially where the railway crossed the road leading to Southend and Machrihanish, although even so the sharpest curve still had a radius of 5·4 chains. The deepest cutting was 28 ft., and the highest embankment 6 ft. There was only one underbridge on the line, of 20 ft. span formed by 4 rolled steel joists with cross timbers and concrete abutments.

Leaving Campbeltown the line climbed a sharp 1 in 33 gradient to cross a ridge, which it descended at the same angle. It has often been said that the railway then followed substantially the track of the old canal but in fact they were for the most part separate, apart from a section about 740 yards long to the south of (Old) Blanchfield. After the descent it ran on an almost level route to Machrihanish. An early article commented on the steep gradient that "By this the length of the line is somewhat shortened, but the more serious evil of curtailing the power of the locomotives is introduced".

There were no stations in the ordinary sense of the word, the line starting on the open quay at Campbeltown and finishing in a field at Machrihanish, although at the latter terminus a small waiting-room was later erected. A number of "Halts" were listed, although these were no more than cross roads, most trains stopping at any cross roads on request. There were actually ten level crossings, all ungated, 3 of which were of public roads and 7 of private roads. Cattle guards were provided at them all to prevent animals straying on to the line.

It was reported in some early reference books that there was no signalling; the Light Railway Order, however, required that wherever trains may "cross or pass one another there shall be a home-signal for each direction at or near the entrance points". In accordance with this signals should have been provided at Lintmill, but in 1910 a Board of Trade Inspector investigating an accident merely commented that, for "one non-stop train in each direction per day . . . a man is provided at the Lintmill passing place to hand to and receive from the driver the train tablet", this function otherwise being dealt with by the guard. On the other hand the Board of Trade's Inspecting Officer reported prior to the opening of the passenger line in 1906 that "At Lintmill passing place is a raised ground frame for working the points and signals . . ." Also an article in the "Locomotive Magazine" two months after the line opened said that at the crossing with the Southend and Machrihanish road out of Campbeltown "there are gates and a signal, which are attended to by a woman."

The short spur at Limecraigs, at the Campbeltown end led to sidings, a reversing triangle, and the "engine depot" and carriage sheds. The latter were simple buildings used to house the motive power and passenger "cars". The approach to these sidings and sheds was a steep down gradient of 1 in 50 entered *via* a left-hand turnout with points facing trains coming from Machrihanish. The yard also contained facilities for fuelling and watering the locomotives.

Two-lever ground frames were provided at the junctions of the siding to the New Quay, the colliery siding between Campbeltown and Lintmill, and the colliery siding near Machrihanish. There was also a similar ground frame for the points of the run-round loop at Machrihanish. The frame at Lintmill had 8 working and 2 spare levers.

The building of the line was not without incident, for local feeling was not one hundred per cent in favour of the project. Indeed when the ground was being surveyed for the Limecraigs cutting, one local landlord carried out an assault on the engineer concerned, for which he was duly charged —only to reply with a counter-charge of trespass. Although it had been hoped to open the line for passenger traffic by the end of 1905 it was actually the summer of 1906 before the work was sufficiently complete for a Board of Trade inspection. Lt.-Col. E. Druitt inspected the line and reported on 21 August that subject to some minor provisions he was satisfied. The qualifications expressed were that cattle guards should be provided at all 7 private road crossings—which had not then been done; ballasting on the down gradient between Limecraigs and Hall St. was not complete, and the speed limit on this section should be fixed at 5 m.p.h.; the rodding and locking apparatus at the facing points on the quay at Campbeltown required boxing in; buffer stops were required at the Machrihanish terminus; some fencing on the old line needed repair; and finally, until ballasting was complete the overall speed limit should be 15 m.p.h. Col. Druitt concluded his report: "Subject to the above remarks I can recommend the Board of Trade to sanction the use of the above railways for passenger traffic."

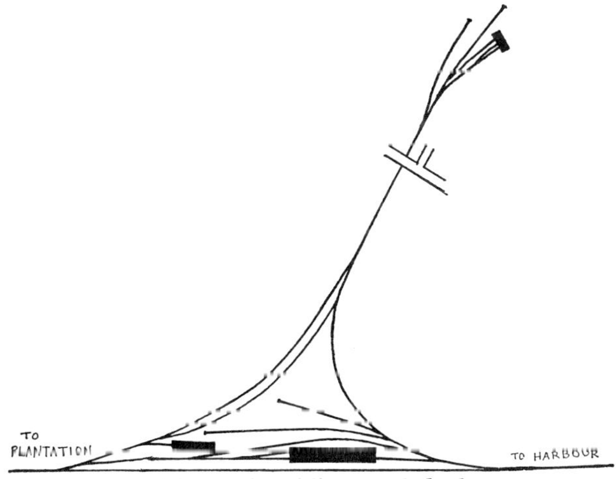

Limecraigs sidings and sheds
Loco shed left, carriage shed centre, coal depot top

Chapter 4

Twenty-five Years

Excursions daily you will see
From the Salt Pans unto the Quay,
Then blythe and merry we shall be
When seated on the railway.
The Campbeltonians when they please
May sit and sail in't at their ease,
And only pay a few bawbees
For a hurl upon the railway.

The Beginning

Inhabitants of Kintyre who paid their penny for the *Campbeltown Courier* on Saturday 18 August 1906 read of Col. Druitt's inspection of the line on the 16th, and how he had "travelled on the rear step of the carriage examining the permanent way as the train proceeded". That there was still some opposition to the railway was evident by the concluding letter of a slightly acrimonious correspondence on the subject, which appeared in the same issue. "Delighted," wrote that he believed "that the Campbeltown and Machrihanish Light Railway will in the future do great good to our town and district." He went on to refute the criticisms of a previous correspondent ("Verb sap") that the railway would be "dangerous" and "cheap and nasty", and even suggested that the Council start a "Common Good Fund" to advertise the amenities of the district.

Meanwhile Col. Druitt had authorised the Railway to open "forthwith". The *Courier* stated, "We understand there will be no formal opening ceremony, but the trains will proceed to carry passengers at once." In the same issue was a report that "The train ran to Machrihanish today in connection with the turbine steamer." This presumably referred to Friday 17 August. It has been suggested that a few days earlier a "special" had been run for the miners and their families, who had to help when it became derailed, but the local press makes no mention of this.

A week later the *Courier* said that "the system has been inaugurated with success, and the only thing to regret is that this modern means of connecting the two shores of the peninsula was not completed before the tail-end of the summer season". The first few days had clearly been successful, for "Last Saturday local folks in considerable force travelled to Machrihanish . . . and at times the carriages were completely filled.

That was the railway's busiest day." It was later reported that during the first three weeks of operation 20,000 people "journeyed over the line", and "the success of the scheme is, therefore, prodigious". This figure related to single journeys and therefore indicated 10,000 individual passengers. It also included a party of "newspaper representatives", who were entertained to the trip.

Great things were anticipated and the *Courier* reported that, "Some people are just now seeing visions of a Kintyre with railways running north and south and east and west." Reality took hold, however, for the report continued: "It is to be feared that such dreams are wholly vain. Nothing less than an industrial revolution in the district could make such a scheme at all feasible. . . . The fact is that but for the presence of coal in the Laggan of Kintyre the present railway would probably never have been thought of." For the present, however, the railway had come, and looked set fair to flourish.

SERVICES

The first timetable to appear in *Bradshaw* showed three trains a day in each direction on weekdays, and three more each way on a Saturday, thus setting the pattern for two characteristics of the train services throughout most of the life of the line. Until 1930 practically every time-table showed extra trains on Saturdays and there was never any Sunday service. The following year saw two more timetable innovations. During the winter months the timing of the Wednesday mid-day down train and its return journey (normally only allowing 10 minutes for the turn round) was put back by 80 minutes and the return train given a prolonged stay of 40 minutes at Machrihanish. The other innovation was a summer train which "Connects with Turbine Steamer and does not stop at halts." The ordinary train stopped, by request, at "Plantation, Moss Rd., Lintmill, Drumlemble, Machrihanish Farm, and Trodigal if required", the guard signalling to the driver from the train whenever a ticket for an intermediate stop had been sold. Other destinations were recognised, although not mentioned in the timetable; for example, the author possesses a ticket from Campbeltown to Moy Park (at the minimum fare of 3d. return). The "express" ran most summers up until the war in 1914 and again spasmodically thereafter up to and including the final timetable in 1931. The exact purpose of this "express" non-stop schedule is hard to see, other than possibly impressing the tourists for prestige purposes, for the nominal timing was 30 minutes, exactly the same as almost every other passenger train that ran over the 25 years of operation. Indeed, apart from the 3 p.m. down train which was timed at 35 minutes from 1930 on, the nominal duration of journey never varied. In some peak years during the summer the "express" was followed out of Campbeltown by an unscheduled single-coach stopping train which, after swopping engines at Machrihanish preceded the "express" back.

One characteristic of the timetables was the large number of exceptional services—trains which ran on certain days only, or except on certain days, or with exceptional stops. There are, over the years, not less

CAMPBELTOWN
AND
MACHRIHANISH
LIGHT RAILWAY

Frequent Trains run between Campbeltown and Machrihanish Golf Links.

Time occupied, Twenty minutes.   Return fare, 1/-

Season Tickets for Fourteen
days and upwards issued
at Greatly Reduced Rates.

Special Trains can be arranged for on Moderate
Terms.

ALEX. BLACK, Superintendent,
Railway Office, CAMPBELTOWN.

than twenty-two different coded entries of this sort in *Bradshaw*, varying from the simple "Saturdays only" to "Mondays, Wednesdays and Fridays only" and "except Tuesdays and Thursdays". From 1920 onwards some trains ran only on school days and in 1907 the very early morning down train (5.50 a.m.) ran "to colliery only". One unrepeated experiment during the period 1908–9 had the early morning departure from Machrihanish listed: "Runs if required on giving notice the previous day."

As the line developed the winter services changed little, but in the summer months the original "Saturdays only" trains soon became a daily service and the number increased slightly so that by August 1913 there were seven trains each way daily with an unbalanced Saturday evening down train leaving Campbeltown at 10 p.m. The war naturally led to a curtailment of services, with the stopping of the Turbine Steamer trips, until the early months of 1917 saw the line's minimum service of one daily train in each direction with three Saturdays only and one Mondays, Wednesdays and Saturdays only from Campbeltown, and one Mondays only and two Saturdays only from Machrihanish. After the war there were problems enough for any railway and in Kintyre troubles in the coal industry were reflected by eight years of timetables showing trains which "Will not run when colliery is idle." On the other hand the tourist trade soon picked up again and before long the summer months saw eight regular trains a day in each direction plus odd Saturdays only workings as well as specials, for by now the company advertised that, "Special Trains may be arranged for on application at Railway Office." It has even been suggested that the normal 4-coach, 256-seat train could be hired for a mere 10s., although this story is a little too unlikely even for the western highlands, and is strenuously denied by the then-manager. Certainly specials did help to swell the coffers and upon at least one occasion the army used the railway to move an entire Territorial unit—men and baggage—into camp at Machrihanish.

Although the 20's saw increasing competition from buses, the timetables continued to show eight trains daily in each direction right up until the withdrawal of services in 1931—and these still included the daily "Express" which, at that time allowed the tourists a full 35 minutes at Machrihanish for their money!

When the railway finally closed the prime reason was the loss of revenue following the closure of the colliery in 1929, but a major factor was also the bus competition. To meet this second-hand buses had been bought by the railway, but the experiment was to no avail and they were soon sold to the competing road transport concern.

Working Methods and Accidents

When the passenger service opened in 1906 it was at first worked with an undertaking to use one engine in steam (or two coupled together) together with a train staff. In fact the Board of Trade's Inspecting Officer approved the use of a tablet *in lieu* of a staff, as it was intended that the line would be equipped with an electric table system "in course of time". And "in course of time" Tyer and Company's "absolute automatic tablet instruments" were duly installed, with instruments at (1) Machrihanish, (2) the colliery siding, (3) Lintmill passing place, for the Machrihanish section, (4) Lintmill crossing, for the Campbeltown section, (5) Limecraigs sidings, and (6) Campbeltown. The instruments were so connected electrically that a tablet could be withdrawn for a particular section of the line at any of the three instruments in the section provided that no other tablet was out from either of the other two; also a tablet restored to any of the three instruments in the section caused the needle on the other two to show "Line clear". The "tablet stations" were all linked by phone and there was one key available which could irregularly release the instruments in a section without a tablet being replaced, and this was normally kept in the possession of the Superintendent of the Line. It was to be the misuse of this key that would later cost a man's life. There were no signalmen and the tablet instruments were worked by the train guards, except for the one non-stop "express" a day in summer, when a man was provided at Lintmill passing place to hand over to, and receive the tablet from the driver.

The locomotives and coaches were said to have been regularly turned on the reversing triangle at Limecraigs, thus causing considerable annoyance at Campbeltown pier with car No. 6, which had the loading doors of the parcel compartment on one side only—and this would frequently be the side opposite that on which luggage had been stacked for loading; if this was so it must also have caused irritation at Machrihanish when the doors ended up facing away from the "platform". The trouble was said to be aggravated by No. 6 frequently being marshalled in the middle of the train. It is, however, true that most extant photos of the passenger trains show the locomotives with their chimneys facing Machrihanish, and photos showing car No. 6 generally show it with the loading doors facing north as the train entered Machrihanish, so perhaps the turning was less frequent than has been suggested. It is true, however, that the train engine involved in the 1910 accident was running chimney first into Campbeltown.

In theory the tablet working of the line in two sections, in the manner described, should have been foolproof, but even the best system of single-line railway working is potentially hazardous, and every system is subject to failure of the human element. The C. & M. was no better than any other line in its strict attention to correct working, and a great deal more care-free than most. As P. B. Whitehouse has said in his "Narrow Gauge Album", "The men of the Western Islands and those of Kintyre have an affinity in that they are remote from the world and too far distant to be worried by petty authority; so it was with the railway, whose operating methods were reminiscent of the West of Ireland."

The very first railway accident in Kintyre had occurred back in 1876, six months before the colliery line opened. The report in the *Campbeltown Courier* is worth quoting in full: 'On Thursday, one of the trucks on the new railway now being constructed between the town and the Coal Works, at Drumlemble, was upset by coming in contact with a cow which had strayed on to the line. There happened to be some boys in the truck at the time, and they were thrown out, but fortunately did not sustain very serious injuries. The animal which belonged to Mr. Alex. Weir, flesher, Longrow, was killed on the spot."

It was not long after the start of passenger services that the line's most notorious—and sadly, fatal—accident took place on 9 August 1910. A passenger train from Machrihanish collided with a stationary engine in the Limecraigs sidings and killed a cleaner, who was knocked down and run over by the engine upon which he had been working. An inquiry was ordered by the Board of Trade and on 2 September Lt.-Col. E. Druitt, the same Inspecting Officer who had sanctioned the use of the line for passenger traffic four years earlier, presented his report to the Assistant Secretary of the Board's Railway Department. It revealed a happy-go-lucky atmosphere amongst the staff, in sharp contrast to the discipline of the Caledonian Railway from which three of the five men involved had come. There was no one villain of the peace, four of the five participants being to some extent culpable of irregularities in working. The unfortunate victim was entirely blameless and unsuspecting.

On 25 July a new timetable had come into operation whereby the 5.10 p.m. train from Machrihanish, after unloading at Campbeltown returned to the sheds, where the cars and engine were put away for the night before the 6.30 p.m. train from Machrihanish passed the sidings. The driver of the 5.10 train was the first on duty the following morning, to take out the 5.50 a.m. train from Campbeltown, after which there was not another train until 9.00 a.m. As the batteries of the tablet instruments required constant attention Alexander Black, an ex-Caledonian Inspector and the superintendent of the line (who was also acting as guard on the 6.30 train) had authorised the working of the line up until 9.00 a.m. each day on the principle of one engine in steam, and with the electrical tablet operation suspended. In order to do this the guard of the 5.10 train was handed the superintendent's key which would irregularly release the tablet apparatus. After the points at Limecraigs had been operated for putting the train away for the night, and then reset to allow the 6.10 train to pass, the tablet was not replaced in the instrument but put in a locker on the engine so that the driver could operate the points in the morning without "setting the electrical signalling in operation". As this left the indicator at Lintmill showing section blocked the guard would then irregularly release the instrument at the sheds with the key, so as to show the Lintmill–Campbeltown section as clear. This by-passing of the system was of course a rash business, but the guard of the 5.10, William Black, who was also assistant superintendent ("I had no previous railway experience") found himself on arrival at Campbeltown with "a lot of enquiries regarding parcels &c., to attend to and . . . some writing to do". Consequently as he had done on "several previous occasions" he sent Norman O'May, a 16-year-old odd-job boy back to the sheds as guard on the train and, as the time the "bedding down" operation normally took was 5 to 10 minutes he "allowed about a quarter of an hour to elapse and relying upon the points being closed as usual" he then released the magnet in the Campbeltown instrument, thereby clearing the section from Lintmill and went off duty. On the day in question, however, the lad, as he testified, "went away for the night along with the driver Harper, but omitted to close the points before doing so. I forgot all about it." Harper, the driver referred to, who was an ex-Caledonian Railway driver testified that "after doing a little work on my locomotive I left for the night along with the boy Norman O'May. The boy usually tells me he has put the tablet on my engine for the morning trip, but that night he did not, and I did not think of asking him about it."

The trap was set and the 6.30 from Machrihanish ran straight into it. James Laing the driver (also an ex-Caley man) saw, from about 20 yards away, that the points were wrongly set but, despite his travelling at no more than 8–10 m.p.h.—due to both the steep down gradient and the presence of children playing near the level-crossing above the points—he was not able to stop. Here again fate played a strange hand for the vacuum brake was inoperative and the rails were greasy at that point "on account of the engines frequently standing there when getting water". The lack of a vacuum brake was due to it having "got out of gear" after the engine had made the outward journey with "a leaky tube". The superintendent, Alex. Black, had consequently authorised Laing "to come on with steam and hand brake only". Even so the collision could hardly have been averted for, with engine brakes and the last two carriage brakes full on the engine skidded down the hill with locked wheels on the greasy rails for about 100 yards until it gently struck the stationary engine at a speed estimated by Laing as no more than 2 m.p.h. The front buffer castings of the train engine were slightly cracked and no damage was done to the carriages. "But unfortunately the standing engine was being cleaned by cleaner G. Jamieson, and he was knocked down and run over by it with fatal results."

The accident was occasioned by a series of irregularities and, as Lt.-Col. Druitt commented, "shows the necessity of always working in accordance with rules." He went on to say, "the irregular method of releasing tablets, which took place for a fortnight, cannot be too much condemned, and should on no account whatever be permitted. I am informed by the Company that it ceased at once after the accident."

Whether irregularities of working remained "ceased" is another matter, for it was said locally that not long afterwards a coal train ran away under similar circumstances—fortunately without anyone being hurt. Runaways were by no means unknown, especially when "Chevalier" was used to replace "Princess" as reserve passenger engine, for she had no vacuum brake but was nevertheless occasionally used to draw the single coach that formed the winter train. On at least one occasion she broke away from the coach while descending the western side of the hill and an accident was only avoided by the engine keeping full steam on (in order to stay ahead of the coach) until a level stretch was reached. It was, however, on the slope down into Campbeltown that runaways were most often seen—especially with the heavily loaded and under-braked coal trains, more than one of which ran into Hall Street to pull up only just short of the façade of the Royal Hotel. As if uncontrolled speed was not enough, the drivers met the competition of the buses when it came by frequent races to see who would be first to the crossings. The train was usually the faster, with estimated speeds of up to 40 m.p.h. (despite the 20 m.p.h. overall speed limit).

There can be no doubting the happy and carefree spirit of this western outpost of the iron way, but it was undoubtedly pure luck that kept the casualty list so low.

—And a Few Memories

Memories of "the old days" tend to vest things with characteristics as varied as the people recalling them, but it is quite surprising with what uniform affection the "wee train" is remembered by those who knew it. Memories reported by others or told to the present author, whether from men or women, ex staff, local residents or day trippers, all recall the happy atmosphere and attractive appearance of Britain's most isolated railway—an atmosphere summed up by one lady who ended her letter, telling of her childhood memories of the C. & M., by saying, "This is not much information, but it has revived happy memories for me." Happy Memories: these indeed seem to be the essence of the railway.

"The happiest days she ever lived were those as 'Nan of the Train'," said one Campbeltown lady, to an inquirer in 1947. Nan—or Nanny as she was more familiarly known locally—was a combined conductress, shuntress and porteress for much of the earlier part of the passenger line's existence. Passengers knew her as the lady who passed along the cars issuing tickets, but she was also familiar with the line in winter, and with the coal trucks as well as the attractive passenger cars. For the last ten years of the line's existence her functions were performed by an equally able successor, "Margaret of the train". But perhaps the man who, more than any other, *was* the railway in the increasingly lean years after the war was Ed. McCabe, the superintendent of the line from 1915 onwards. Known as "Wee McCabe" he was the only person on the line to wear a uniform and, although "wee" in stature was not so in any other way. Like his predecessor Alex. Black, "Wee McCabe" had to be a man of many talents. He it was (despite conflicting stories linking the episode to "Nan") who, when the line was flooded by heavy rain, raised steam in the only available locomotive—the ancient "Chevalier"—and drove it to the rescue of the train marooned to the west of the swollen Chircan Burn. He it was, too, who enrolled his family to help on the railway during the busy periods. One tale tells of a young son earning his pocket money by riding on the front buffer beam of engines used to assist heavy trains up the sharp gradient, so that at the top he could lean over and uncouple, thus allowing the light engine to run back to the harbour without the train having to stop. Ed. McCabe often acted as conductor. On the school trains the scholars had a very healthy respect for him, and there was no rowdyism when he was on board. When conducting and ticket collecting, he blew his whistle for the train to start and indicated to the driver, by a show of fingers, the next stop. One day in the holidays some children were playing in a field beside the railway when the boat train came along. Just as the train was passing it suddenly came to a stop and a man in plus-fours was unceremoniously bundled out by Mr. McCabe. The train went off, leaving him waving and shouting on the line and the children beat a hasty retreat, as anyone who had suffered such treatment from "Wee McCabe" must have been a villain indeed. This was the train returning to Campbeltown, so the miscreant would miss the boat and have to stay the night.

The scholars' train was often conducted by lesser lights, and one of these was known as "Dauntless". He was a good-natured lad who got a lot of tormenting about his cap, which was a light tweed one and always seemed to be too big for him. The carriages were lined with varnished wood and under the windows there were holes about the size of a penny at regular intervals, presumably for ventilation. The children used these holes to dispose of waste paper, toffee papers, old school exercises, etc. One night coming home a bright spark dropped a lit match down one of the holes and soon smoke was emerging, first from one opening and then right along the compartment. The alarm was raised and the train stopped. After consultation between the crew "Dauntless" disappeared, to return in a few minutes, truly dauntless, with a lemonade bottle full of water, which he poured solemnly, a little at a time, down each hole. In due time the smoke ceased and the train continued with the scholars, no sadder but perhaps a trifle wiser. Occasionally, on longer stages, "Dauntless" would disappear, and then word would be passed round from observers at the front that he was having a "shot" at the engine.

The main engines were, of course, "Atlantic" and "Argyll", but the older one was put on in emergencies, usually in winter when the others were having their overhaul. The children loved these occasions, for sometimes the train would not start in the mornings from the Town and other times it refused to leave Machrihanish. If it was on time, there was always the hope that it would stick on Narrowfield Brae. Sometimes it would slip back and take a second or third race at the hill. It got slower and slower until it finally surmounted the top in triumph and slid down the hill on the other side. The result of this was that the scholars were sometimes late for school, but they walked in with very smug faces and a complete alibi which made them the envy of less fortunate schoolmates who needed no conveyance.

The mother of one schoolgirl used to make up rhymes and parodies to amuse her children. One favourite ran something like this:

> "There's a loud loud voice a-calling,
> Are the scholars out of bed?
> For the time is swiftly flying
> And the clock is not ahead.
>
> Get your boots and scarves and jumpers
> For the North wind's got a nip,
> And hurry! or you'll find that train
> Has given you the slip."

The train did not often give them the slip (or they it). Their station was "The Bridge", but on very wet or stormy mornings they would go to "The Gate", which was nearer. One morning, this lady recalls, she was late and ran to "The Gate" but the train got there first and flew past. She turned for home but suddenly heard a long whistle and looking round found the train coming backwards along the line. Someone had seen her plight and she didn't get a holiday after all.

On another occasion it was her sister who held the train up. The rest of the children were safely in their seats and she was flying through the field. Suddenly she stopped, bent down and the began retracing her steps and performing the most peculiar looking antics. After a bit she came running on and finally reached the train. She explained that the ball of wool from her school sock had jumped out of her bag and she didn't notice till brought up by a jerk. She didn't break the wool but, being conscientious and a good Girl Guide, she carefully retraced the wool over and under the grass and round each thistle, until she found the ball. Never was anyone scolded for these escapades—everyone seemed to take them with good humour.

The carriages were divided into two compartments with a glass-panelled door between, which was always kept locked. The same scholars always travelled in the same compartments and between the front end and the back there was almost constant feud, and also occasional fights within each compartment.

One of the drivers was a very good athelete and when the old engine was in use he used to get out and run alongside for a spell. He was also a very good shot with a lump of coal and more than once brought down a rabbit in the Dalivaddy Moss. He would jump from the engine, over the fence, collect his kill, and be back in his place in a matter of seconds.

It was, of course, the summer visitors who provided most of the passenger traffic. Visitors like the lads of the 103rd Coy. of the Boys Brigade from Ibrox who camped at a farm near Machrihanish. One of those "lads" remembers 60 years later how, only a few years after the railway opened, they would walk to Machrihanish, over the sand dunes, to catch the train to Campbeltown for a meal before walking back. Despite the lapse of time this "lad" said in a letter to the author. "This is a memory in my life that I have never forgotten." Presumably those boys didn't know the public house at one of the rail-road crossings, called "The Hungry Hoose", a *soubriquet* earned when it was the only one of the several public houses on the road from Campbeltown to Machrihanish which did not serve oatcake with the dram.

The granddaughter of James McMurchy (the poet who penned the verses heading these chapters) tells of her happy memories of sailing from the Broomielaw at 6 a.m. on the "Davaar", captained by Peter McFarlane—the famous "Para Handy"—to spend her summer holidays with her grandfather at Machrihanish. The long sail around the islands terminated at Campbeltown at 2 p.m., with a train "connection" leaving at 3 p.m. and stopping at every crossroads on the way.

Day trippers, too, had fond memories of the line. One lady remembers holidays spent sailing about the Clyde with her father, and the Campbeltown trip kept until last as a special treat. Often they would take the train to Machrihanish. "We had just time to enjoy the sight of the big Atlantic rollers," she says, for the turbine steamer would be "a law unto itself as far as connections were concerned; as we found to our cost more than once."

Happy memories indeed, of a happy-go-lucky railway in a land where the bustle of life has never made over-much impression, and time was the servant, not the master, of man.

A fine old postcard view portraying an early train for Machrihanish near Kilkerran Crossing. *Lens of Sutton*

A down train passing along the foreshore in 1906. *J.G. Steel*

A four coach passenger train with *ARGYLL* in charge, emerging from Limecraigs cutting in 1906. This was the "Golfers express". Just behind the engine was the site of the carriage shed. *T.M. Haddow*

An early 1900's view of *CHEVALIER* at the Colliery (with crew) showing well the sparse footplate and controls. *Courtesy of Model Railway Constructor*

A latter view of *CHEVALIER* (minus nameplate) showing the revised chimney, springing, buffers, 'homemade' cab etc., and the conversion to 0–4–2 arrangement. *Ken Nunn Collection, L.C.G.B.*

Two further views of the colliery engine *CHEVALIER* outside the engine shed in
May 1925 showing clearly the home made cab.   *Real Photographs*

A view of *ATLANTIC* being prepared for service on the 26th April 1922.
Ken Nunn Collection, L.C.G.B.

A side view of *ATLANTIC* showing engine detail.
Ken Nunn Collection, L.C.G.B.

ATLANTIC locomotive seen here with full steam pressure outside the Argyll photographic studios in Hall Street at Campbeltown in August 1930.

H.C. Casserley

ARGYLL in fine condition showing the full livery, with the Company crest, name (in shaded lettering) and brass maker's plate.   *Real Photographs*

The diminutive locomotive *PRINCESS* built by Kerr-Stuart in 1900. This view shows the livery on the side tanks and photographed at the Colliery.
Courtesy, Model Railway Constructor

A view after scrapping of *PRINCESS* showing the rear cab details well.
Ken Nunn Collection, L.C.G.B.

Two further views in May 1925 of the scrapped *PRINCESS* which show more constructional details of the locomotive, as well as a good variety of wagon stock (*lower photograph*). The wagons on the left are a large coal wagon and milk wagon.   *Ken Nunn Collection, L.C.G.B. and Real Photographs*

Seen here at Machrihanish in August 1930; the locomotive *ATLANTIC* with parcels car No. 6 (*next to engine*) on a passenger train for Campbeltown.

H.C. Casserley

A three coach passenger train with No. 6 coach in the centre at Machrihanish in 1907. The station building is on the extreme left. *T.M. Haddow*

Hall Street, Campbeltown in 1929 with the three coach nearing departure.

W. Anthony

A small view of Limecrags sheds and sidings. On the left is the water crane, *ARGYLL* shunting wagons in the centre, coaling stage, engine shed, small wagons, carriages and carriage shed on right; finally the mainline.   *W.J. Anderson*

With coach No. 1 and No. 4 plus two other coaches, *ARGYLL* has a fully loaded train in 1906.   *Real Photographs*

0–4–2ST *CHEVALIER* in charge of a heavy train of hutch carriers.

W.J. Anderson

Two views in 1906 of *ARGYLL*; both trains heavily laden. The lower photograph is believed to have been on the occasion that F. Moore painted his colour view of the engine and stock; the reference used for the railway's livery. *Real Photographs*

Both *ARGYLL* and *ATLANTIC* pressed into service with this heavy six-coach pasenger train.   *Ken Nunn Collection, L.C.G.B.*

ARGYLL at Campbeltown in August 1930, with coach No. 1.   *H.C. Casserley*

A postcard of the 1920s with a posed and "retouched" view of *ARGYLL* and four coaches.

Lens of Sutton

The official crest of the Campbeltown & Machrihanish Light Railway Company.

Oakwood Press

...RGYLL with a train in 1906 ...out to cross the main road. ...ote the Trespass notice on the ...ght, and the colliery in the ...ckground. *W.J. Anderson*

...RGYLL at Hall Street in ...06. *J. Caple*

...RGYLL at Hall Street at the ...ad of the Steamer Express. *H.C. Casserley*

ARGYLL at Hall Street, Campbeltown in August 1930, again with the Steamer Express, with coach No. 5 leading the four coach set and No. 6 at the rear.

H.C. Casserley

ATLANTIC with a two coach train passing the lattice signals at Lintmill Halt.

Ken Nunn Collection, L.C.G.B.

A busy scene at Campbeltown with *ARGYLL* outside The Royal Hotel in August 1930, presumably the steamer having just docked. *H.C. Casserley*

Two timetables for the line, *top* 1911 Bradshaw's, and *bottom* 1922 Bradshaw's.

CAMPBELTOWN and MACHRIHANISH LIGHT.

Miles.		Week Days only.												Miles.		Week Days only.											
		mrn	mrn	aft	Sats.	aft	aft	aft	Sats.	aft		Sats.					mrn	mrn	Sats.	aft	aft	Sats.	aft	aft	Sats.	aft	Sats.
	Campbeltown ¶ ....dep.	5 50	1020	1 0		2 10	4e20	6 0		9 20	...	...			Machrihanish ¶ ...dep.	8e40	1110		3 5	4 40		5e10	6 45		1015	
6	Machrihanish ......arr.	6 20	1050	1 30		2 40	4e50	6 30		9 50	...	...		6	Campbeltown ......arr.	9e10	1140		3 35	5 10		5e40	7 15		1045	

e Except Saturdays.   ¶ "Halts" at Plantation, Moss Road, Lintmill, Drumlemble, Machrihanish Farm, and Trodigal if required.

CAMPBELTOWN and MACHRIHANISH LIGHT.

Miles.		Week Days only.														NOTES.
		c	mrn	d	aft	aft		aft	Sats.	aft						
	Campbeltown ¶ ....dep.	6 0	1020	1 10	3 0	4 20	....	6 30	{	9 45	...					
6	Machrihanish ......arr.	6 30	1050	1 40	3 30	4 50	....	7 0	{	1015	...					¶ "Halts" at Plantation, Moss Road, Lintmill, Drumlemble, Machrihanish Farm, and Trodigal if required.

Miles.		Week Days only.												
		h	mrn	d	aft	aft		aft						
	Machrihanish ¶ ...dep.	8 10	11 0	2 15	3 45	5 45	....	7 30	...					
6	Campbeltown ......arr.	8 40	1130	2 45	4 15	6 15	....	8 0	...					

c Does not run when Colliery is idle.   *d* Does not call at **Halts**.   *h* Runs on School Days only.

Side view of *ARGYLL* at Campbeltown, 1930.   *H.C. Casserley*

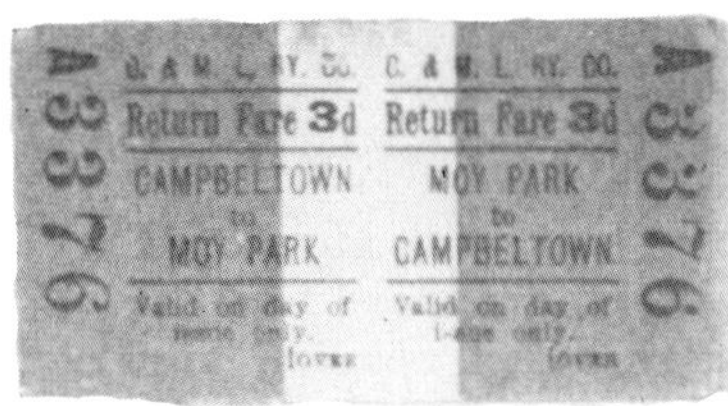 

 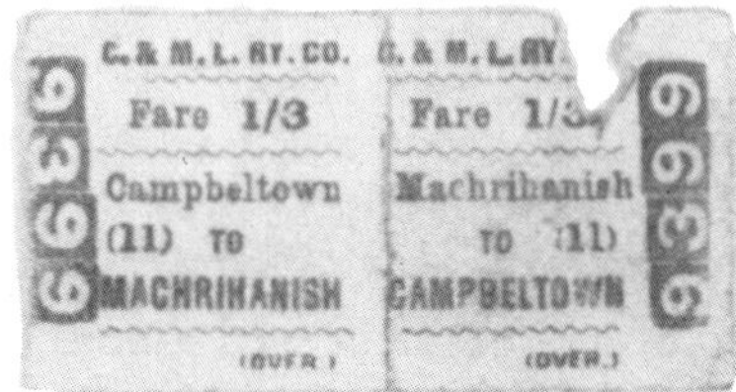

A selection of tickets of the C. & M.L.Ry.Co.

ARGYLL on a four-coach train at Machrihanish in the 1920s.
R.W. Kidner Collection

Chapter 5

The Financial Side

Success unto these gentlemen
Shall echo loud from hill and glen,
For our conductors weel do ken
How to lay a railway.

Finale

Unfortunately almost all the company's papers were long since destroyed and the only facts that are available to substantiate the tale of how the railway flourished—more or less—are gleanings from *Bradshaw's Shareholders' Manual and Guide*, which ceased publication in 1923, and odd annual reports which have survived. Almost miraculously a consecutive set of these telling the tale from 1915 to 1924 is in existence, but little remains of the records of the other years.

At first the financial year ran from 1 August, and the early years certainly approached the hoped-for prosperity. As has been recorded, some 10,000 passengers used the line during the first three weeks of operation, and also at that time the coal trade was thriving. The first year of working showed a profit, and a dividend of $2\frac{1}{2}$ per cent was declared with the sum of £250 being transferred "to reserve". The following year, the novelty apparently having worn off a little, the dividend was down to 2 per cent with nothing going to reserve. For the next three years there was no dividend, although sums of £250 (1908–9) and £500 (1909–10) were paid to reserve. In 1911–12 and 1912–13 a dividend of 2 per cent was shown, with a further £200 to reserve in the latter year as well as £229 19s. "carried forward". In 1913 the financial year of the company was altered to coincide with the calendar year, a balance of £268 being carried forward after the 5 months' working up to 21 December of that year, and this seems to mark the beginning of the downward trend. The report of 31 July 1913 recorded the watershed of the company's finances and thereafter there were to be few dividends, and a balance sheet which was kept viable almost entirely by the sums carried forward year by year and built upon that first operation in 1913.

The war naturally affected traffic, although these effects were less than might have been expected. Sailings on the Clyde virtually ceased for other than strictly necessary purposes, yet for the year ending 31 December 1916 the Directors were able to report that "The continued stoppage of the Turbine Steamers has affected the Company's earnings, but these are £251 better than last year. The increase is wholly on the passenger train service." The war led, however, to the same evil on the C. & M. as on the main-line railways—a drastic reduction in routine maintenance, and this could not continue unchecked. In 1917 sums had to be expended in necessary arrears of maintenance while in 1918 the amount available to "carry forward" reached an all-time low of £69 16s. 10d., due to increases in wages and the cost of materials.

Following the war the pattern perversely changed. Passenger services expanded as tourists again came "doon the watter" but the mineral traffic took a shaking from the labour disputes of the early and mid 20's. Time-tables between 1920 and 1925 regularly had the early morning trains marked as "will not run when colliery is idle". The position was worsened for the railway at this time by the increasing competition from local bus services which, while taking away little of the tourist trade, made considerable inroads in the indigenous passenger traffic, as the buses passed through all the villages, which the train did not. Despite all this the company managed to pay a 3 per cent dividend from 1922 to 1924, but the writing was on the wall.

Just how small and tight a budget the railway was working on may be seen by some of the figures from the 1921 annual report—which also gives an indication of the low wages of the day and the proportions of various types of traffic carried.

The administration was the cheapest department of all:

Directors' fees	Nil
Secretary's salary	£100

Income from passengers and goods carried came to £4,575. This was made up of:

	£	s.	d.
Ordinary passengers	2,761	0	0
Season tickets (workmen)	102	0	0
Mails	6	7	6
Parcels	479	0	0
Goods receipts	1,227	0	0
	£4,575	7	6

Maintenance costs on the locomotives and rolling stock were low:

		£	s.	d.
Locomotives	Wages	105	0	0
	Materials	352	0	0
		£457	0	0
Carriages and wagons	Wages	—		
	Materials	126	10	10

TABLE 1. SUMMARY OF ACCOUNTS

1915–24

	Railway																								Extra Receipts			Total Gross Income			Rentals, etc.			Interest on debentures			C/F			Dividend per cent
	Gross receipts			Expenditure			Net receipts																																	
	£	s.	d.	£	s.	d.	£	s.	d.	£	s.	d.	£	s.	d.	£	s.	d.	£	s.	d.	£	s.	d.																

Year	Gross receipts £	s.	d.	Expenditure £	s.	d.	Net receipts £	s.	d.	Extra Receipts £	s.	d.	Total Gross Income £	s.	d.	Rentals, etc. £	s.	d.	Interest on debentures £	s.	d.	C/F £	s.	d.	Dividend per cent
1915	1620	13	6	1337	16	5	282	17	1	31	0	0	313	17	1	173	14	0	300	0	0	236	19	10	0
1916	1871	18	8	1331	14	10	540	3	10	35	10	4	575	14	2	173	14	0	300	0	0	338	19	11	0
1917	2495	4	3	2200	19	4	294	4	11	37	4	2	331	9	1	173	14	0	300	0	0	196	15	0	0
1918	3309	12	6	3021	5	8	288	6	10	51	12	1	339	18	11	166	17	1	300	0	0	69	16	10	0
1919	4756	2	11	4102	12	2	653	10	9	36	10	0	690	0	9	123	14	2	300	0	0	336	3	5	0
1920	5181	13	5	4770	11	0	411	2	5	71	9	8	482	12	1	123	14	2	300	0	0	395	1	5	0
1921	4574	17	5	3917	6	9	657	10	8	117	3	1	774	13	9	139	14	7	300	0	0	730	0	7	0
1922	4408	11	3	2955	11	4	1452	19	11	89	15	2	1542	15	1	123	14	0	300	0	0	1149	16	10	3
1923	4044	17	3	3197	7	6	847	9	9	136	11	4	984	1	1	123	14	0	300	0	0	1011	4	7	3
1924	3719	4	8	3121	1	8	598	3	0	148	19	5	747	2	5	123	14	0	300	0	0	635	10	6	3

The running costs of the locomotives came to a greater figure, of course:

		£	s.	d
Wages ..	.. ..	501	13	8
Fuel ..	.. ..	987	13	7
Water ..	.. ..	8	2	6
Lubricants ..	.. ..	84	5	3
		£1,581	15	0

At this time there were three locomotives in service—"Argyll", "Atlantic", and the old "Chevalier". In 1923—a fairly typical post-war year—the mileage run showed that the passenger services accounted for substantially the larger side of the business:

Coaching miles run			14,790
Goods miles run	2,609		
Goods miles run empty	2,609		
		——	5,218
Total engine miles run			21,383

These figures show a surprisingly high number of miles run as "light" engine, or with empty stock trains—1,375 for the year in question. For a railway of less than 6½ miles in length this was quite a feat, and is probably accounted for by the unbalanced late down train each night which had to run back to the sheds at Limecraigs empty. Although the balance sheets mention miles run with empty goods trains this figure is not recorded for empty passenger trains.

It is also worth noting that for the year referred to above (1923, the year of the grouping of the standard-gauge lines) the amount of coal carried came to 21,373 tons.

In the earlier years the coal traffic had been the backbone of the line, the basis upon which it relied for financial stability, but following the labour troubles of the early twenties very little coal was mined after 1926 and large numbers of Kintyre folk left the district, the mining tradition in many families being finally broken after several generations. The pit struggled on until 1929 when, in that September it eventually closed. The financial loss to the railway, which had been operating on the very slenderest of margins was disastrous, despite the continued popularity of the service with the tourist trade. Coming on top of the loss of indigenous passenger traffic to motor transport (at the time the line opened in 1906 there had only been seventy-five motor cars registered in the whole of Argyllshire) it was more than the company could stand. For a short while the line struggled on and in 1931 hopes were briefly raised when the Maisels Petroleum Company was floated to re-open the pit and distil oil from the coal. Moneys were raised for this project and some of the wagons were even repainted, but alas it was a false hope. The scheme fell through and in November, the tourists having all gone home, services were withdrawn.

CLOSURE

As the fortunes of Kintyre deteriorated during the bad years of the depression so it seems did the scope of local news coverage given by the *Campbeltown Courier* and unfortunately very little information about the railway's closure is to be found in its columns (although there is lengthy reporting of the struggles of the rival bus company of A. & P. McConnachie to obtain a licence to cover the same route). The result is that no exact closure date is known, and the railway's final year or two of existence are wreathed in mists of uncertainty.

In the early June of 1931 the financial pressures were clearly becoming obvious, with the pit having been closed for nearly two years. The *Courier* commented that "June day trippers have not been difficult to count so far. On Monday two people were seen making for the Machrihanish train, and a sarcastic individual at the corner remarked—'Their ticket must hae come up!'" At that time the train had been running again for less than a week after five months during which the company had, from 27 December 1930 to 1 June 1931, attempted to run their services with two second-hand buses. These "red" buses were not very popular locally, especially as there had been a period in the February when they had broken down and there were neither trains nor buses running. Local support was more behind the "blue" buses of Messrs. A. & P. McConnachie who had been running on the same route, although without any authority to do so. Matters reached a peak at a sitting of the Traffic Commissioners for the Southern Scotland Traffic Area, at Greenock on 17 July, which was reported in the *Campbeltown Courier* a week later. At this sitting Messrs. McConnachie were applying, amongst other things, for a licence to run a Campbeltown to Machrihanish bus. The application was "strenuously opposed" by the Light Railway Coy., whose "precarious position" was "brought to light". McConnachie argued that there was a demand for their services, they served "three villages that were untouched by the railway", and that, "There was absolutely nothing to support the contention of the Railway Company that the railway could adequately supply the district." The solicitor representing the railway counter-claimed that everything said by the appellant's solicitor "in favour of his client's buses must apply to the railway buses". He further declared that, "It was a matter of life and death for the Railway Company that they should be allowed to maintain this service. It was in order to save their lives that they put buses on the route. That was the only expectation the Railway Company had of saving the £30,500 of capital that had been sunk in the railway." He went on to claim that the railway had the advantage in terms of both comfort and safety, as well as an obligation to "serve the workmen". Great stress was put on the possible future of Kintyre. "If there was any chance of a revival of the colliery, the need would arise for conveying the workmen to the pit. There was also the goods traffic, and the railway had the plant ready to meet that demand. Similarly if there was any question of a new industry between Campbeltown and Machrihanish, the railway was in a position to serve its needs." It was also pointed out that the "three villages" served by the blue buses were one of only about 20 cottages (Drumlemble) and two small hamlets.

In reply, the solicitor for Messrs. McConnachie was blunt and to the point. "The position really was that the Railway Company put the old horse vehicles off the road, and now the motor buses were putting the Railway Company off the road. The railway was dead no matter what feelings they might have in the matter. The Railway Company were asking the impossible in seeking to save £30,000 of capital off two buses." And so the case rested until the Commissioners' decision was made known. It was a bombshell to the Kintyre people when the decision was announced —in favour of the railway.

"Widespread indignation and resentment," was the mood reported by the *Courier* of a meeting held in the Territorial Hall, Drumlemble, on 17 August. This meeting was held in support of "Messrs. McConnachie's appeal against the decision to the Minister of Transport, Mr. Herbert Morrison". About one hundred people turned up and expressed their feelings in no uncertain manner. One Machrihanish man said, in the course of "a rousing speech" that "the people of the district were getting a more efficient service and greater courtesy on the road from Messrs. McConnachie, than they had got when the railway was running". He also commented adversely on the railway's fare increases which had been made to combat falling passenger revenue. He claimed that the railway "now only served a summer trade". He went further and stated that, "If the railway was out of date it was high time it was scrapped like any other piece of machinery. Instead of scrapping, however, they had placed on the road those red buses. He advised the people to travel by the blue buses. Let the railway keep to the railway." A Drumlemble man then spoke of the school-children who, although the railway had the school contract, "travelled by bus, and he thought they had no intention of going back to the train". He went on to paint a pitiable picture of the poor children's suffering in inclement weather and then proposed a resolution protesting against the Commissioners' decision and seeking its reversal. The meeting was gradually becoming more acrimonious and references were made to the Ministry of Transport's "laxity" and "acting in a blindfolded manner". The last speaker suggested that "if people were determined to have Messrs. McConnachie on the road, to support their petition they could surely 'pad the hoof' for a while and sicken the other crowd. . . . This concluded the business of the meeting."

Certainly 1931 was not a successful or happy summer for the railway, which carried virtually only the excursion traffic. It was not prepared to die however and struggled on gamely for a few months. Trains were certainly running in mid-September and it was not until November that the last public timetable appeared in *Bradshaw*.

When the summer trips began again in 1932 the lack of a railway in Kintyre was noticed by the local paper as if for the first time. The *Courier*, reporting the arrival of the T.S. "Queen Alexandra" on its first trip of the season said, "For the first time since the Campbeltown and Machrihanish Light Railway was opened the 'wee train' failed to greet the arrival of the turbine steamer for the opening of the excursion season with its once familiar whistle. The railway is out of action and the question is if it is to be numbered among the local glories now departed. The Machrihanish run in connection with the steamer excursion was taken by motor "buses". "*Ichabod*" indeed, for less than two months later the railway's office in Hall Street was taken over by McConnachie's bus company as a goods and parcels office and the trains never did run again.

If the closing of the line was an uncertain and indeterminate affair, the legal obsequies at least were mercifully brief. A notice in the *London Gazette* of 14 November 1933 announced a meeting of creditors called for the 21st. It was clear that matters had gone well beyond any hope of redemption and an extraordinary resolution was passed: "That it has been proved to the satisfaction of the Company that this Company cannot, by reason of its liabilities, continue its business, and that it is advisable that the same should be wound up; and that the Company be wound up accordingly.

That Herbert Edward Hill, Chartered Accountant, of 19 Coleman Street, E.C.2, be and he is hereby appointed the Liquidator of the Company." A notice dated 24 November required all creditors to submit their claims by 30 December 1933, and so the company passed into oblivion.

The land, plant, wagons, etc., had already been sold to a scrap merchant in the previous June. The three engines were broken up on the spot, while the coach bodies were taken the following year to Trench Point to serve as holiday cabins.

The railway had opened without ceremony, and thus it faded away—rather than closed—some 54 years after the first steam-hauled coal train ran into Campbeltown.

Conclusions

The Campbeltown and Machrihanish Light Railway was a line which would have had a happier ending but for matters outside the company's control. Basically depending upon a mineral traffic with a history of some 450 years of increasing prosperity, the passenger service was a gamble with the unknown; yet in the end it was the passenger service which remained viable and the colliery trade which unexpectedly disappeared. Like all narrow-gauge railways the C. & M. was designed for low-cost running, small turnover, and a slender profit margin. The loss of revenue from the mineral traffic was a body blow from which it could not hope to recover and, coupled with the spread of the internal combustion engine, brought about an untimely closure after only 25 years of passenger working.

Could the line have had a future if the pit had remained open? Probably it could have continued running until after the second world war, when road traffic competition came to force the closure of much more important and profitable routes. In 1945 the pit was re-opened and was subsequently developed by the National Coal Board but, despite suggestions that a railway should be relaid, it was road transport which proved the economical way of moving the coal.

Now the pit is again closed—probably for good. Kintyre has lost its collieries and its distilleries and is entirely an agricultural and tourist centre. Little remains of the railway except the Limecraigs cutting, and "Atlantic's" whistle and a few tickets in the Campbeltown Museum. The track is barely distinguishable and at Machrihanish there is a new housing estate where the terminus once stood "by the shores of the Atlantic".

Just one further thing remains of Scotland's only narrow-gauge railway —the very happy memories of long ago.

Chapter 6

Locomotives and Rolling Stock

With locomotive swift and strong
Upon the line we'll dash along,
The people they will quickly throng
To see our Hielan' Railway.
The moorland folk will run wi' fricht,
And hide themselves far oot o' sicht,
Sayin' "Tougal, run wi' a' your micht,
Auld Nick is on the railway."

When the Colliery railway opened in 1876 there was only one locomotive, an 0–4–0 tank engine named "Pioneer" built by Andrew Barclay of Kilmarnock. She had 24 in. to 27 in. diameter driving wheels (the exact size is not known) with a 4 ft. wheelbase and inside frames. This latter point of design on a narrow-gauge engine naturally led to a narrow grate and lower part of the firebox, with the upper part of the firebox widened out. This in turn meant that when the firebox needed renewing it could only be removed by taking out the end of the boiler, which would otherwise have been unnecessary. Subsequent locomotives had outside frames and parallel-sided fireboxes to overcome this time-consuming nuisance. It was also found that the four wheels on a short (4 ft.) wheelbase caused trouble with the permanent way. The engineer, Mr. T. L. Galloway, reported that, "On rough parts of the road their jolting was excessive, and the hammer-like action of the wheels soon aggravated any imperfections of the permanent way, and caused the rails to bend and fish plates to break." To cure this a pair of 15 in. wheels was mounted on a radial truck beneath the cab, thus "preventing damage to the permanent way, and at the same time adding to the comfort of the engine-drivers".

Unfortunately no pictures of "Pioneer" have come down to us, but a verbal picture has been drawn by James McMurchy, the crofter-poet of Kintyre, at the time the railway first opened.

Hark! there she's comin' doon the brae,
Along by Crossel Hill,
A train o' waggons close behind—
I hear the whistle shrill.

> Go spread the news through a' the toon
> Wi' joy the news they'll hear;
> Oor hielan' line is open noo—
> There comes the "Pioneer".

The "Pioneer" had a hard life and virtually went out of service after "Princess" appeared in 1900. She was reported as "stored away at Drumlemble" when the Light Railway Company took over in 1906, and her final fate is not known.

The longest-lived locomotive on the line was "Chevalier", originally an 0–4–0 saddle tank with a 2 ft. $4\frac{3}{4}$ in. diameter boiler and outside frames and cylinders, built by Andrew Barclay in 1885 for Messrs. J. and T. L. Galloway's Argyll Colliery Company. She was assembled at the works in Kilmarnock and then unbolted and dismantled, shipped out in sections and re-erected in Campbeltown. This locomotive was also the one with the most varied appearance. As originally supplied "Chevalier" was an 0–4–0 with 2 ft. diameter wheels, but her short wheelbase (4 ft.) was, like that of "Pioneer", not kind to the track and to spread the weight a pair of 15 in. trailing wheels was added making her an 0–4–2. She was later rebuilt in 1926—in a rather amateurish fashion—by the railway company, using parts from the younger "Princess". In original condition "Chevalier" had an open cab with no rear bunker or back plate, a tall stove-pipe chimney and large square wooden buffers firmly fixed to her wooden buffer beams, rather like the over-riders on a car bumper. The rebuilding consisted of refashioning the cab by cutting the side plates straight down in line with the front plate, moving the structure forward and adding on the bunker and rear of the cab from "Princess". She was also given a new chimney, "Princess's" sandbox (mounted on the near side of the running plate, forward of the boiler) and central Norwegian type buffer/couplers at each end. The old wooden buffers were removed but the original wooden buffer beams were retained. As originally supplied "Chevalier" was smartly painted, apparently in black, with double white lining, carrying a cast name plate on each tank side and the makers' works plate on the cab side. Both plates disappeared with the rebuild, however, and the old girl gradually achieved a nondescript dirty "colliery" appearance far removed from her smart turnout when new. No vacuum brake was ever fitted, despite which "Chevalier" was occasionally pressed into use for passenger service, especially in winter when the trains consisted of only one coach. The old engine was still in use when the line closed and was listed amongst the assets of the company when it was finally wound up (in 1933) at the age of 48 years.

"Princess" was the only locomotive in Kintyre not built by Barclays.

TABLE 2. PRINCIPAL DETAILS OF LOCOMOTIVES[1]

Name	Maker	Works No.	Type	Date built	Wheels Driving	Wheels Trailing	Wheelbase Coupled	Wheelbase Total	Overall Length[2]	Width	Cylinders
					ft. in.	ft. in.	ft. in.	ft. in.	ft. in.	ft. in.	
PIONEER	Barclay		0-4-0[3] 0-4-2[4]	1876 (1875)	2 0 to 2 3	1 3[4]	4 0	7 0			
CHEVALIER	Barclay	269	0-4-0 ST[3] 0-4-2 ST[4]	1885 (1883)	2 0	1 3[4]	4 0	8 9	14 0[3] 16 4¼[5]	6 0[3] 5 10[5]	7 in × 15 in. o.c.
PRINCESS	Kerr-Stuart	717	0-4-2 T	1900	2 2 (2 3)	1 4	3 0	7 0 (7 8)	14 0	6 6	
ARGYLL	Barclay	1049	0-6-2 T	1906	2 9	1 10	6 4 (6 7)	12 9 (12 11)	20 7½	7 2¼	11½ in × 18 in. o.c.
ATLANTIC	Barclay	1098	0-6-2 T	1907							

NOTES: 1. All locomotives had outside frames except "Pioneer".
    2. Over buffer beams.   3. As originally built.
    4. As altered.   5. As rebuilt, in 1926.
N.B. Some dates and dimensions are uncertain. In these cases both alternatives are given and the less certain one placed in brackets beneath the more probable figure.

She was an 0–4–2 side tank engine built by Kerr-Stuart of Stoke-on-Trent to a standard design, and was perhaps the most attractive engine on the line, with a distinctly "Emmet"-like appearance. Built for the colliery in 1900 and delivered within 7 weeks of the order being placed, "Princess" was taken over by the C. & M. Lt. Rly. Coy. in 1906. She had 2 ft. 2 in. driving and 1 ft. 4 in. trailing wheels and a 3 ft. coupled wheelbase with outside frames, bearings, cranks and cylinders. Overall—excepting her standard buffers—she measured 14 ft. in length and 6 ft. 6 in. in width. When the new company took possession in 1906 "Princess" was chosen—as the newest of the colliery engines—to be the reserve passenger locomotive and fitted with a vacuum brake and Norwegian type central buffer/coupler. She was unlined and carried her name painted on her tank sides in 4 in. high letters. The small cast works plate was affixed low down on the tank sides below the front of the cab. When finally her boiler could last no longer without major attention she was withdrawn in 1926 and cannibalised to modernise "Chevalier", which took over her duties.

For the opening of the new passenger line the Company ordered a smart new tank engine from Messrs. Andrew Barclay. Although made to fit the 2 ft. 3 in. gauge of the line the new locomotive had its frames made so that a subsequent widening to 2 ft. 6 in. was possible "should that course prove desirable for any reason". This was doubtless at the request of T. L. Galloway, the engineer, who was on record as being troubled by the lack of "some authoritative standard gauge" for narrow-gauge railways, which would allow the more ready production of "standard" narrow-gauge designs of locomotives and rolling stock.

The new engine was a great advance on anything seen in Kintyre before. The wheel arrangement was 0–6–2, with 2 ft. 9 in. coupled wheels and 1 ft. 10 in. radial truck wheels with a transverse play of $1\frac{1}{2}$ in. in either direction, controlled by check springs. The coupled wheelbase was 6 ft. 4 in., and the total wheelbase 12 ft. 9 in. Outside cylinders were employed, $11\frac{1}{2}$ in. diameter $\times$ 18 in. stroke, and the engine was fitted with Walschaert's valve gear. The boiler barrel measured 9 ft. $\times$ 3 ft. and contained 86 tubes of $1\frac{3}{4}$ in. diameter; there was a total heating surface of 354 sq. ft., a grate area of 8 sq. ft., and the working pressure was 160 p.s.i. The water tanks held 600 gallons and the coal bunker 15 cwt. Unladen the engine weighed 17 tons and laden 20 tons 10 cwt. It was fitted with a vacuum brake and central spring buffers and couplings as well as standard buffers.

The new locomotive—works No. 1049—was delivered about June of 1906 and proved entirely satisfactory in operation; so much so that another identical model was ordered for the summer season of 1907. The first

0–6–2 was named "Argyll" and carried its name in large letters on the side tanks as did its younger sister which was called "Atlantic" and had the works No. 1098.

The two new engines were painted in an identical style to that in use on the North British Railway, that is in the colour officially described as "dark gamboge" with lining in black with thin vermilion and white lines. "Dark gamboge" is actually a colour which is not recognised by artists. In his history of the North British Railway (1955, Ian Allan) C. Hamilton Ellis, himself a railway artist of the highest reputation, comments that if one attempts to darken gamboge by adding black it turns olive green, and this may indeed account for the later published description of the locomotives as being painted olive green, around 1914. The Campbeltown and Machrihanish engines were frequently in need of a good cleaning and the black grime on top of the gamboge would give an olive-green effect. Certainly there is no evidence of them having ever been repainted. The names were painted on the tank sides in large gold letters blocked blue and red, *à la* North British. At the rear of the tank the makers had affixed their large oval works plate of cast iron with a green painted background, and to the forward end was a crest—the arms of Campbeltown in a band bearing the words "Campbeltown and Machrihanish Light Railway Company", and surmounted by a North British 4–4–0 locomotive *sans* tender. Just why a railway such as this short narrow-gauge line should include a standard-gauge tender engine on its crest is not clear.

These two smart new locomotives were responsible for almost all the passenger workings until the line closed in 1931, after which they were eventually broken up for scrap.

THE PASSENGER CARS

The Company had ordered their passenger coaches from the firm of R. Y. Pickering and Co., of Wishaw in Lanarkshire. When the new line opened there were four bogie "cars" in service, and a fifth and sixth were delivered very shortly afterwards. The "cars" were designed by John J. Pickering, son-in-law of the firm's owner, and were externally very attractive models of the tramway type, 43 ft. 6 in. long and with two 4-wheel bogies, 30 ft. centre to centre carrying 1 ft. 11 in. diameter wheels. At each end was a covered platform, guarded by a wrought-iron balcony and "telescopic gates", and with steps on either side to within a foot or so of the ground, so that station platforms would not be necessary. They carried the firm's nameplate on the frames.

Internally the "cars" were divided by a transverse central partition and had a central corridor between transverse rows of slatted wooden seats with reversible backs, providing accommodation for 64 in each "car". The fittings were Spartan with unlined planking on the roof and walls: alternate windows had an upper inward-opening section for ventilation. Lighting was no less primitive, although brackets were provided to hold the candles that were the sole illumination.

Car No. 6 differed from the others, being a composite passenger/parcels vehicle. A quarter of the interior length, in the centre, constituted the parcels van, which had no windows; a pair of ordinary hinged doors were fitted on one side only.

The external finish of the "cars" was olive green for the lower panels and cream on the upper panels, although in later years the cream colour became more of an "off-white", while the olive green weathered to a dirty brownish-black. The waistband bore the letters "C. & M. L. Ry." in the centre, and "No. 1", "No. 2", etc. (from 1 to 6) at each end. The vacuum brake was fitted and, surprisingly, an early article about the railway stated that "the smoothness of the running is most marked".

The coaches were not broken up when the line closed but were taken to Trench Point in Campbeltown for use as "summer cabins" and later as Naval store-rooms and workshops. Up until 1965 they could still be seen there.

MINERAL WAGONS

Originally coal was taken directly from the pit face in narrow "hutches" which were run directly along the line to Campbeltown, but later bogie transporter wagons were built to carry the hutches—one of the extremely rare example of transporter wagons running on the narrow gauge. These wagons, which belonged to the Colliery Company and were still in use when the Light Railway Company was formed, were of the platform type with short rails laid transversely across them, on which the small colliery hutches containing coal were carried. They had 24 in. wheels and a $4\frac{1}{2}$ ft. wheelbase. How many of the wagons were in use is not clear, but in 1897 the prospectus of the Campbeltown Coal Co. listed, amongst the assets of the old Company which were to be taken over, "18 wagons". Each wagon carried four of the hutches side by side and, on each side of the wagon was a beam, locked with pins, to hold the hutches steady; despite this they still sometimes rolled off. They were also each fitted with a handbrake "which can be fastened down when required". As each hutch carried only $9\frac{1}{2}$ cwt. of coal and their tare weight was $2\frac{1}{2}$ cwt. each, to be carried on an 18 cwt. (tare) wagon the effect was that 38 cwt. of coal was being carried in a wagon weighing 66 cwt. gross; that is, the coal accounted for only $57\frac{1}{2}$ *per cent* of the total load. On the laying of the new line however the Campbeltown Colliery Company soon announced its intention of considering a larger capacity design of wagon in which the loads carried could be increased now that the double-handling at Campbeltown was no longer necessary. Accordingly some 4-ton wagons were acquired from Hurst-Nelson and some of the old flat wagons were built up into 3–3½-ton wagons.

The new 4 ton wagons were timber sided and had a single "door" at one end hinged at the top. The underframe solebars were extended at each end to form dumb buffers, in addition to the Norwegian type central buffer and coupler. It was on account of these dumb buffers that the locomotives had standard buffers in addition to the central Norwegian type, for this was all that was fitted to the passenger stock. Ordinary hand brakes were fitted but no vacuum brake. On each side the wagons carried the letters "C. C. C." indicating their ownership.

Goods Vehicles

When the new line from Limecraigs to the harbour was opened it was found that the steep descent with non-fitted coal wagons often induced trains to run away. Consequently in 1907 a large and heavy goods brake van was obtained by the new railway company, but unfortunately this meant that trains had to include three coal wagons less to compensate and consequently it was usually left in a siding. The van measured 14 ft. over the body length and had 21 in. diameter wheels and a 7 ft. wheelbase. It was fitted with ordinary buffers as well as the central Norwegian buffer/couplers. The timber body had a sliding door and a running board/step at the left hand end of each side—that is in diagonally opposite corners—and two windows in each end. Externally it resembled a parcels van more than a brake van but internally there was a brake screw mounted centrally. It was lettered "C. & M. L. Ry." on each side. After the closure of the railway the brake van ended its days as a hen house.

It appears that the company owned one further vehicle, annual reports in the 20's referring to the stock as "Other Coaching Vehicles—Brake Vans, Milk Wagons . . . 2". Nothing further is known of this vehicle however.

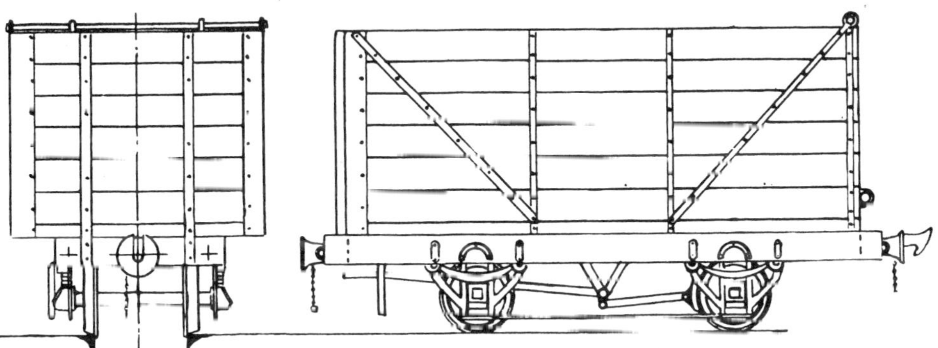

Some Poetry

Apart from the two poems of James McMurchy which appear as Chapter headings, a number of other poems about the railway have appeared, the best of which in the author's view is that reproduced below. It appeared in the *Campbeltown Courier* just three weeks after the line opened in 1906, and was signed simply "C.M."

A Railway O' Oor Ain

The toon, ye'd hardly ken it noo, it looks sae big an braw,
Richt prood they'd be tae see it, them that's been a while awa,
For wi' motor caurs, an a' sich like, we're up-tae-date, that's plain,
An' noo tae cap it a' we've got a railway o' oor ain.

    A railway a' oor ain, nae less,
    A railway a' oor ain;
    Gin ye've yer doots, jist come an' see't,
    This railway o' oor ain.

Jist roon ayont the Auld Quay Heid, an' staunin' on the line,
Ye'll see some bonnie kerriges, a' pented up sae fine;
Noo step ye intae yin o' them, an a' yer cares'll vanish
Afore yer faur upon the road that runs to Machrihanish.

    An' whan yer on the railway wance,
    Ye'll sune be on't agane,
    O' man its gran! the very thocht—
    We've a railway a' oor ain.

Whan the railway first wis spoken o' some folk wad hum an haw,
An' say tae yin anither it wad niver dae at a';
But noo its an accomplished fac' as ony yin can see,
They're jist as keen tae tak their hurl, as aither you or me.

    An' it's railway this, and railway that,
    An' railway ower agane;
    Ye'd think tae hear them blawin' noo
    That the railway wis thir ain.

Ye often hear o' folk gaun oot a jaunt tae the Saut Pans,
An' mony gether there, they say, frae faur aff foreign lands;
Then whit's tae hinner us at hame tae tak the gude o't tae,
Whan the railway runs maist frae the door tae Machrihanish bay.

    An' we'll tak oor freens oot wi' us,
    An' we'll a' gang back agane;
    For it's easy come an' easy go
    On this railway o' oor ain.

An' noo a' maun be stappin', I hae kep' ye faur ower lang.
Ye see I wis sae happy ower the subjec' o' ma sang:
An' whan tae them that's faur awa ye're writin' aince again,
Jist gie them a' the news ye can o' oor braw new railway train.
    Then we'll wish gude luck tae Campbeltoon
    An' may she iver gain
    A routh o' blessings choice and sweet,
    Frae this railway o' her ain.

TICKETS

Only a very few tickets have survived and some of these are badly faded, therefore it is possible to give no more than an outline of ticket design and colours. There was, of course, only one class of travel, and the author has only seen return tickets.

1. Ordinary return. These were yellowish-brown with a broad white central stripe in the earlier days but after the war, when the fare was raised from 1s. to 1s. 3d., they had a white outward half and a yellow return half. Numbers were generally blocked and facing outwards but one early ticket has open numbers both facing to the left, prefixed by the letter "A". Some later issues were printed on white paper and resembled bus tickets.

2. Special tickets. Some tickets were issued in lots of ten for 10s. These had a light red outer half with a narrow vertical yellow stripe in the centre, and a blue return half with a narrow vertical green stripe in the centre. Numbers were blocked and facing outwards.

3. Children's tickets. These were light red with a thin dark red diagonal cross on the outward half. Numbers were blocked and facing outwards.

4. Free passes. These were contained in a mid-green leather cover with gold inscriptions. One side of the cover had the inscription "Free Pass" and the other a representation of a 4–4–0 locomotive *sans* tender (similar to that depicted on the crest). The name of the holder was entered inside and the pass was not transferable. These passes were issued to Colliery Officials and Officers of the Turbine Steamers, as well as to Railway Officials.

ACKNOWLEDGEMENTS

The help of a great many people has been given in the preparation of this book; especially from official sources. It is a pleasure to acknowledge the assistance rendered by the Scottish Record Office and by the staffs of several libraries and reading rooms—particularly those of the British Museum in London, the Mitchell Library in Glasgow, the Scottish National Library in Edinburgh, and the Central Public Library and library of King's College in Aberdeen. The Chief Draughtsman of Messrs. Andrew Barclay of Kilmarnock and the Press Officer of the National Coal Board in Edinburgh have both been very helpful in providing material, as have a large number of private individuals, too numerous to name individually, who have written to relate their memories of the line, or to loan photographs or documents of interest. Amongst these latter people mention must be made of two, Miss Elizabeth Cuninghame who so kindly recalled memories of the school trains and Mrs. Netta Gow who provided copies of the poems by her grandfather, James McMurchy, which are included throughout the book, and gave permission for them to be reproduced. All authors are to some extent indebted to those who have previously touched upon their subject and Mr. Nigel MacMillan of Glasgow, who has devoted many years study to this line and has modelled it, has published a number of articles about the railway which the present author has found of great interest, and some of these have been of value in confirming certain points which were otherwise obscure.

Finally, thanks are due to Microfilm Records (Aberdeen) Ltd. for their very careful work in copying and producing the photographs; Mrs. Sidney Edwards for producing the line drawing of the crest and the layout map of Limecraigs sidings; and Mrs. Kathleen Sangster for her careful preparation of the typescript from the original semi-legible MS.

BIBLIOGRAPHY

Annual Reports of the C. & M. Lt. Rly. Coy., 1915–1924
Campbeltown & Machrihanish Light Railway Order, 1905
Dott, G. "Notes on the history of the Campbeltown & Machrihanish Railway", 1947
Galloway, T. L. *The Campbeltown Colliery & Light Railway*, Glasgow, 1902
Inspecting Officer's Report prior to the opening of the Line, 1906
Inspecting Officer's Accident Report, 1910
Prospectus for C. & M. Lt. Rly. Coy., 1905
Issues of the following periodicals during the relevant period:
 Bradshaw's Railway Guide
 Bradshaw's Shareholders' Manual and Guide *The London Gazette*
 The Campbeltown Courier *The Railway Magazine*
 Coal *The Locomotive Magazine*

Appendix One.
Coaching Stock Drawings

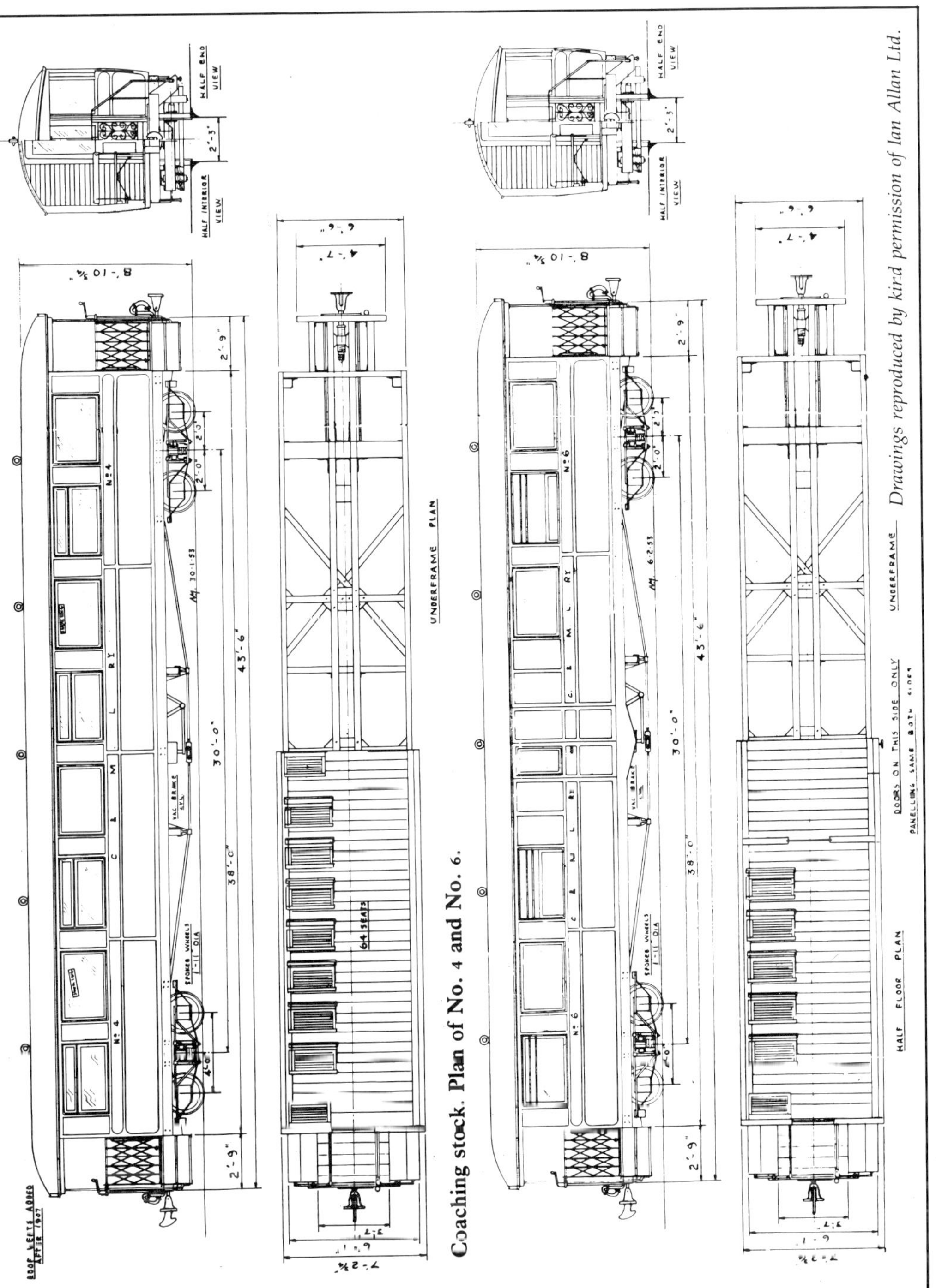

Coaching stock. Plan of No. 4 and No. 6.

Drawings reproduced by kind permission of Ian Allan Ltd.

Appendix Two.
Locomotive Drawings

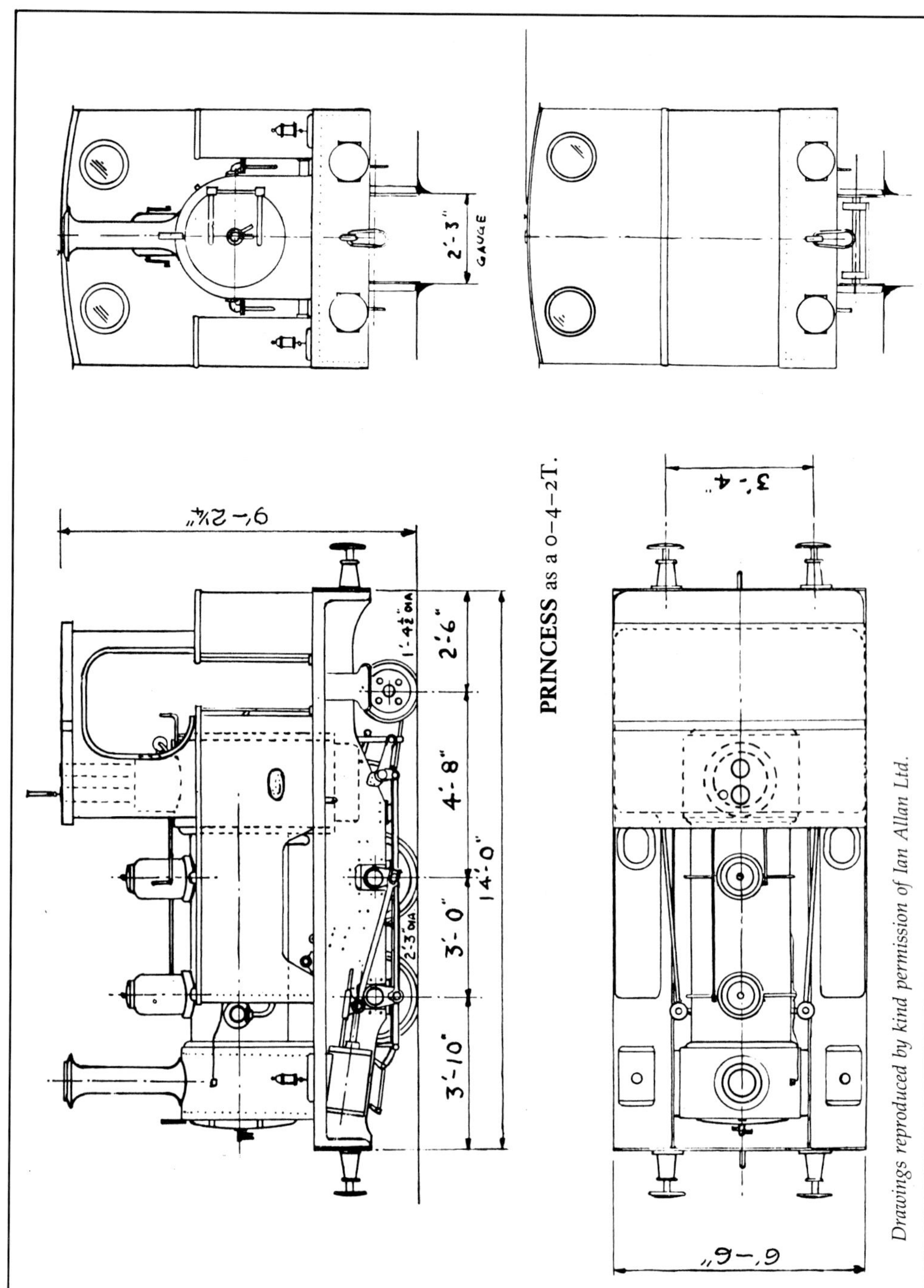

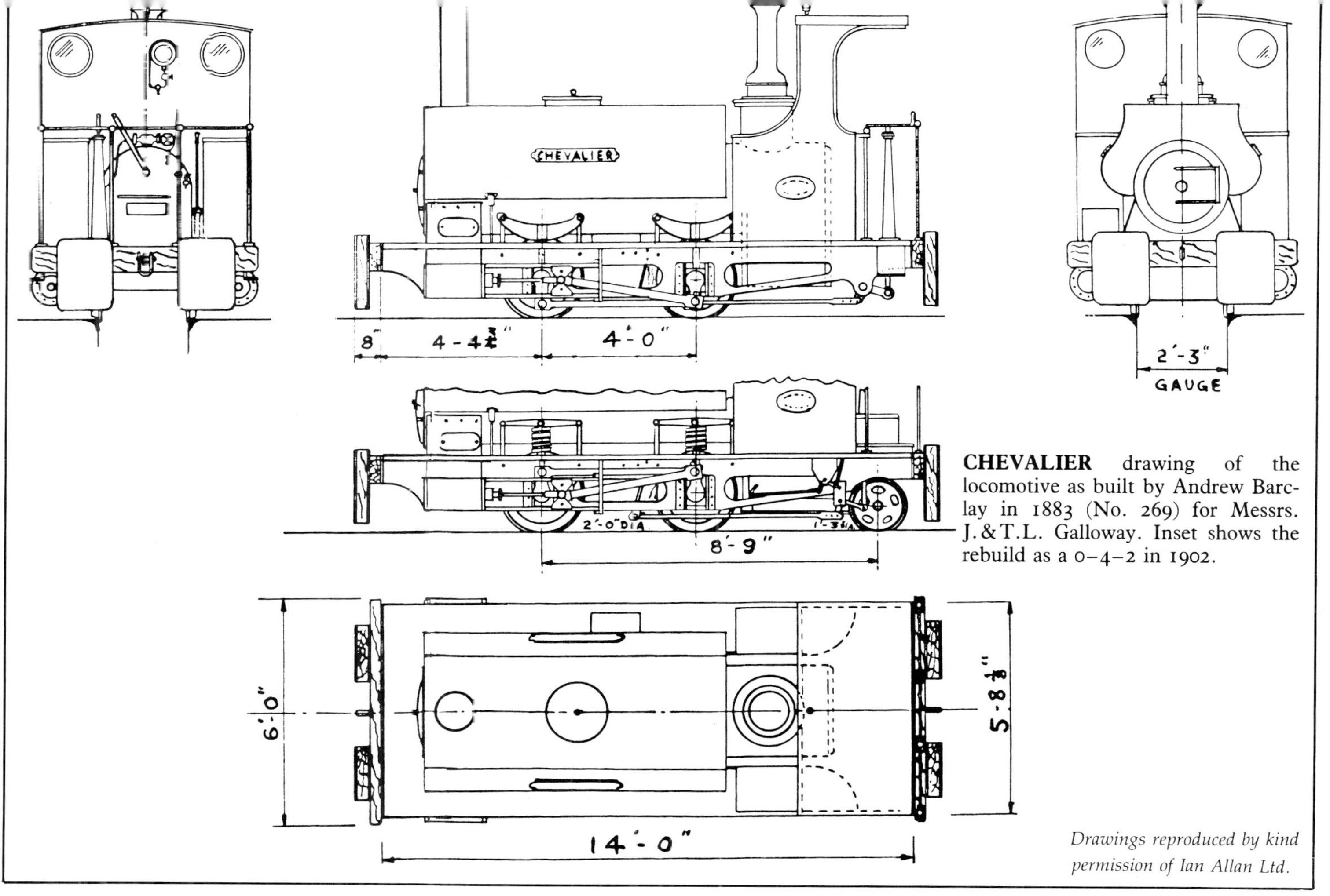

CHEVALIER drawing of the locomotive as built by Andrew Barclay in 1883 (No. 269) for Messrs. J. & T.L. Galloway. Inset shows the rebuild as a 0–4–2 in 1902.

Drawings reproduced by kind permission of Ian Allan Ltd.

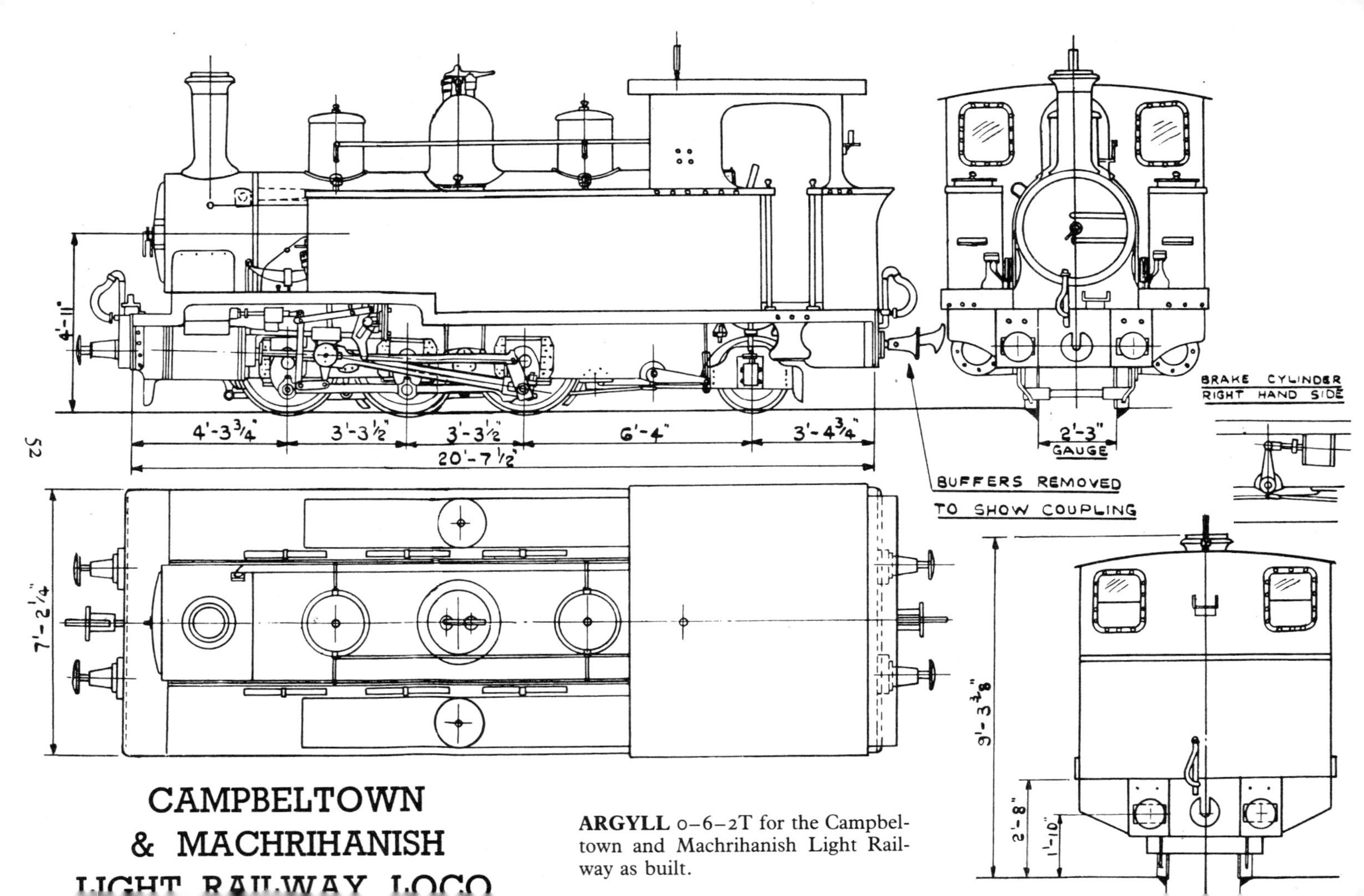
BRAKE CYLINDER RIGHT HAND SIDE
2'-3" GAUGE
BUFFERS REMOVED TO SHOW COUPLING
4'-3¾"
3'-3½"
3'-3½"
6'-4"
3'-4¾"
20'-7½"
4'-11"
7'-2¼"
9'-3⅜"
2'-8"
1'-10"
CAMPBELTOWN & MACHRIHANISH LIGHT RAILWAY LOCO
ARGYLL 0-6-2T for the Campbeltown and Machrihanish Light Railway as built.

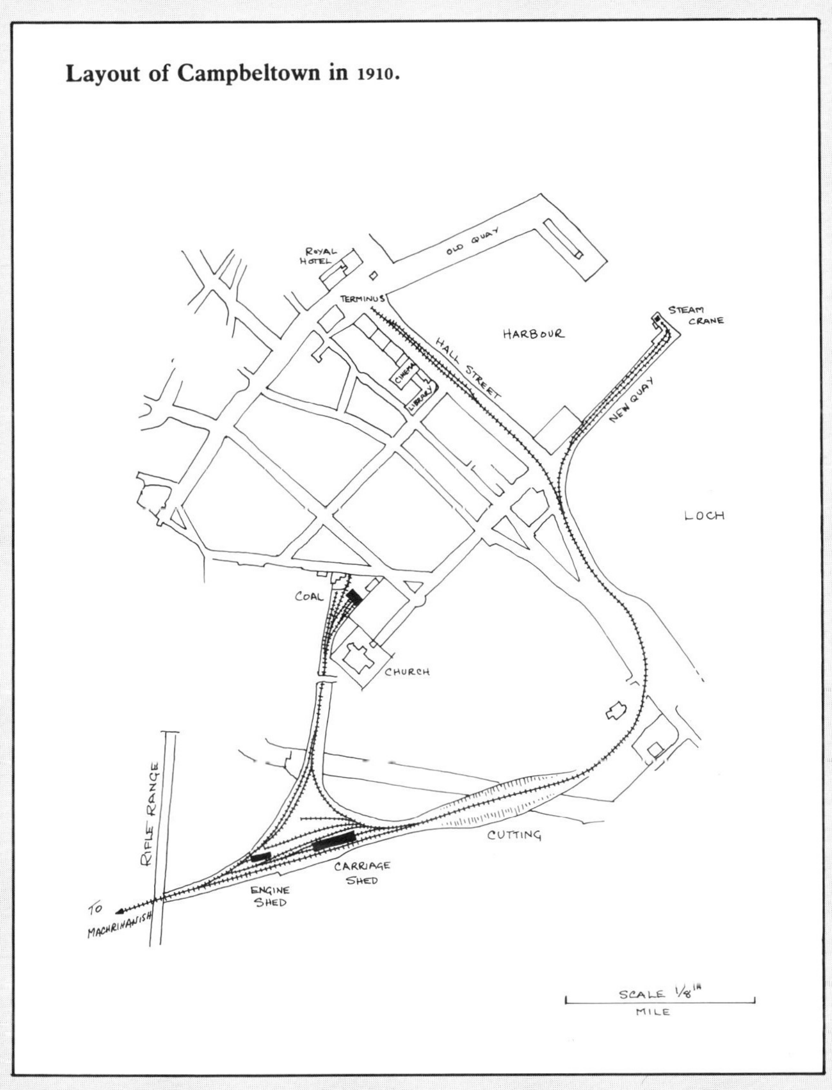

Layout of Campbeltown in 1910.
ROYAL HOTEL
OLD QUAY
TERMINUS
STEAM CRANE
HARBOUR
HALL STREET
CINEMA
LIBRARY
NEW QUAY
LOCH
COAL
CHURCH
RIFLE RANGE
CUTTING
CARRIAGE SHED
ENGINE SHED
TO MACHRIHANISH
SCALE 1/8ᴵᴺ
MILE

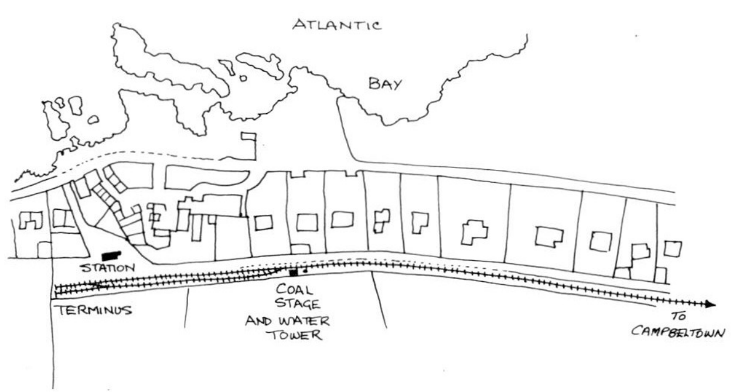

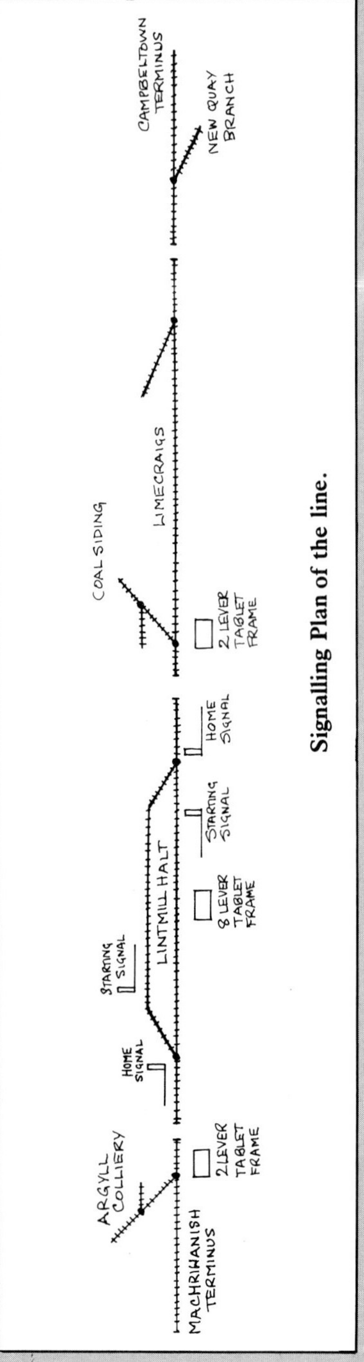

Signalling Plan of the line.

Layout of Machrihanish.

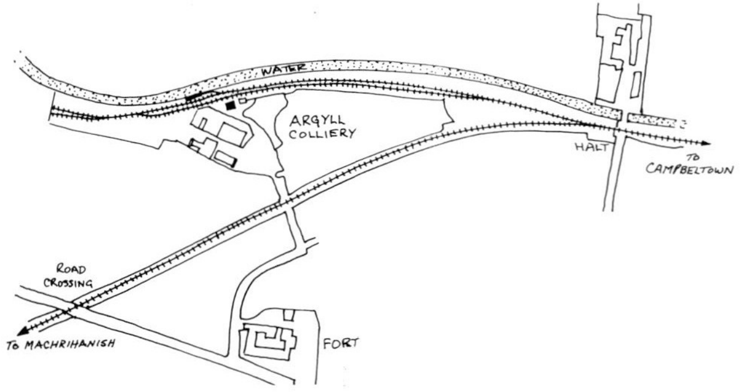

Layout of the Colliery at Argyll.